"One of the most important skills for the '90s is the ability to adapt to and manage change. *On Target* is not only 'a good read' but also shows you how to be in control."

—Pat Harrison, President, AEF/Harrison International

"Hurray! Finally a book that tells you to get it together already and enjoy your life!"

—Dr. Tessa Warschaw, Author of *Winning by Negotiation* and *Rich is Better*

"*On Target* has some powerful and simple messages conveyed to us through stories and images. We learn through the lives of other people about work and life and meaning."

—Anne L. Bryant, Executive Director, American Association of University Women

"As an 'educator' of patients, medical students, residents, and fellows, I can without reservation recommend *On Target* to help you achieve your goals of success and ultimate satisfaction. The author's insights into greater self-achievement are invaluable."

—Dr. Thomas J. Errico, Assistant Professor of Orthopedic Surgery at NYU Hospital

"This book is a must read for anyone who wants to get the most out of life, both personally and professionally. It delivers a powerful combination of motivation and inspiration with a practical step-by-step approach to change, making it one of the most useful and thought-provoking books I've ever read. *On Target* hits it right on the nose for anyone who wants career advancement AND a rewarding quality of life. It is practical, inspirational, and makes you think."

—Mary Berner, Associate Publisher and Vice President, *TV Guide*

On Target is full of wisdom and inspiration for anyone hoping to succeed at a new life challenge."

—Kate White, Editor-in-chief, *McCall's*

"On Target is useful reading. It helps each of us to create of our lives not so much a mosaic, which has separate and distinct parts, but rather a tapestry, in which our personal and professional lives are held together with strong threads.

—Kay Wright, Director of Public Responsibility,
American Express

"This is the best book I've read on attaining a personal vision of success. It is subtle and profound—and a pleasure to read—and will surely have a powerful impact on those seeking to shape their own strategies for succeeding. The authors are astute observers and reporters, making their advise extremely timely and relevant to the '90s. Reading this book will help you discover more about yourself and the world around you—and in so doing you're bound to make some startling connections. This book is credible, sound, and original. It's an important and lasting contribution to the literature of success."

—Scott DeGarmo, Editor-in-chief and Publisher, *Success* magazine

"On Target will find a place in many homes. The book speaks of personal identification, sense of self, goal setting, triumph through action . . . all so important in the '90s. *On Target* makes the destination very clear and attainable."

—Alexandra Lebenthal, Vice President,
Lebenthal & Company

"On Target provides material that has significant 'life's learning' value. It's timing is brilliant. It takes the idea of 'career focus' and 'total life' and shows us how they can work together."

—Judsen Culbreth, Editor-in-chief, *Working Mother*

"On Target is the road map which helps us to understand our cultural, economic and social diversity, and prepares us to take giant steps toward clarifying how we can use this diversity to advance our personal goals."

—Vivian Manning Fox, Executive Director,
YWCA of New York City

"This compendium of advice, wise counsel and gentle nudging aims to meet today's needs and anticipate those of the new century . . . answering the hard questions prompted by declining job security . . . suggesting useful techniques in self development."

—Vincent Audinot, Executive Director,
Guttman Breast Diagnostic Institute

"This book is living proof: The authors have learned how to recapture faith, energy, and success—with practical common sense. *On Target* tells just how they do it."

—Kate Rand Lloyd, Editor-at-large, *Working Woman*

"Jeri and Rick are masters at bringing the best out in people. They help the reader make the transition from mere journeyman to craftsman. You too can do this by putting *On Target* in your life's toolbox."

—Ariel A. Allen, Vice President, Creative Services,
Colgate-Palmolive Company

"Career-minded people take note—if you wish to be confident in your chosen career, this is important reading. If you are uncomfortable or planning a career move of any kind, this could be a lifesaver. Sedlar and Miners's *On Target* should be at the very top of your to-do list.

—Pamela Poff, Partner, Jackson, Lewis, Schnitzler & Krupman

"*On Target* is on-target. It's a must read for anyone who wants a bit extra out of life."

—Walter O'Brien, Executive Client Services Director,
Ogilvy & Mather Worldwide

ON TARGET

ON TARGET

Enhance Your Life and
Ensure Your Success

JERI SEDLAR AND RICK MINERS

 MasterMedia Limited • New York

Copyright © 1993 by Jeri Sedlar and Rick Miners

All rights reserved, including the right of reproduction in whole or in part in any form. Published by MasterMedia Limited.

MASTERMEDIA and colophon are trademarks of MasterMedia Limited.

Library of Congress Cataloging-in-Publication Data
Sedlar, Jeri.
    On target : advance your career and enhance your life / Jeri Sedlar and Rick Miners.
        p. cm.
    Includes bibliographical references.
    ISBN 0-942361-76-8
    1. Career development.   2. Success in business.   I. Miners, Rick.
  II. Title.
  HF5381.S464   1993   93–12656
  650.14—dc20   CIP

Designed by Jacqueline Schuman
Printed in the United States of America
Production services by Martin Cook Associates, Ltd., New York

10 9 8 7 6 5 4 3 2 1

Contents

Introduction   *ix*

PART I / KNOW THYSELF   *1*

1. What Makes You Tick?   *3*

2. Back to Basics: Believing in Yourself   *15*

3. Create Your Own Definition of Success   *31*

4. Setting Your Life Goals   *47*

PART II / YOU AGAINST THE WORLD   *63*

5. Charting Your Course   *65*

6. Focusing on Resources   *79*

7. Aim to Make a Difference   *93*

PART III / YOU AT WORK   *105*

8. How Does Your Job Pass Your Test?   *107*

9. The Art of Networking and Self-Promotion   *121*

10. Winning Traits: What Goes into Making You Stand Out   *135*

11. A Postscript: Putting Things into Perspective   *149*

Suggested Reading   *155*

Index   *159*

Acknowledgements

There have been so many people throughout the years who have touched my life in the most meaningful ways and might not have even been aware of it. Now I have an opportunity to say thank you. As I worked on this book, I recognized thoughts, experiences and advice that others had shared with me. This book has been inside of me for so long that it is such a wonderful sense of fulfillment to finally have it here. For all of you who listened to me talk about writing a book, and wondered if I would ever do it, I say thank you for your support and belief. And to our editor, Jennifer McNamara, a special thanks to you for making the book happen.

This book has been my own journey and along the way I realized just how much we are products of our environment. As we wrote about the importance of optimism, I realized how much I was my mother's daughter—that my optimism came from her. As I thought about the meaning of success and what makes me tick, I realized that my father had given me the value system and the solid beliefs that I have in myself and people in general. I only wish that he were still here to see how I have put my upbringing into practice. And lastly, I wouldn't be the woman that I am today, professionally and personally, if it weren't for my husband. I'm glad that in this big world that we found each other.

—Jeri Sedlar

On Target was a stop on my life's journey. This stop enabled me to commit to paper some of the learnings shared by countless individuals who have assisted me on this journey with directions and detours, good wishes, hope and belief that everything has a meaning and a purpose to someone, if not me alone. Life isn't just work, or play, sadness or joy, anxiety or elation. It is all those things. Through it all, this trip has never been boring, and that is a wish that I make for all of the readers of this book—that they never be bored. Life is exciting, so go out and live it.

My journey began with the love and support of my parents. They taught me many useful things to be used on the journey. The most important thing was to live my life by the Golden Rule—which has been a journey, not a destination.

An important thank you goes out to our editor, Jennifer McNamara, whose ideas, commitment, and editorial expertise made this book possible.

And to Andy Sherwood and my colleagues at Goodrich & Sherwood, thanks! You are great travelling companions.

—Rick Miners

Introduction

During the last ten years, we have traveled throughout the country speaking to people about their careers and their lives. Since the stock market crash of 1987 and the worst recession this country has seen since the Great Depression, people have expressed concerns about their lives that go deeper than the stress brought about by the economy. In the 1980s we saw many people focusing on their careers and often overlooking their personal lives. By the time the '90s rolled around, they began to notice their lives lacked balance and were out of sync. They had compartmentalized their lives and were feeling unsatisfied with the result. Their concern for more balance and more meaning is today shaping the way they see themselves and their careers as they look for definition in a changing world.

As job security becomes less and less a reality for most of the U.S. work force, people are taking stock of their lives in a new way. Now more than ever, people are asking themselves crucial questions: "How can I increase my level of competence on the job? How can I make myself more marketable in the work force? How can I make myself invaluable to an employer?" Unsure of what any career path can promise for the future, they are asking an even more fundamental question: "How can I create a life I'm happy about living?" And even for those of us who are lucky enough to enjoy job security in these hard times, "Is this all there is? How did I get here?" are frequently asked questions.

Our decision to write this book didn't come in a flash. Our

original aim was to write a book on career advancement. Specifically, we wanted to put together a list of career performance tips that we and our audiences have found useful. We discovered very quickly, however, that in the midst of a terrible economy and a changing world, our present-day audiences were asking as many life-oriented questions as career questions. People were in flux, times were changing, needs were changing. Naturally, our ideas for our book began changing, too. Instead of focusing singularly on career advancement, we decided we should begin with the individual and the much broader issue of life enhancement. By beginning with the psychological needs of the individual and funneling down to the practical aspects of an individual's life, we have tried to create a kind of "whole life" handbook.

In setting out to achieve our goal, we have put together the common threads of what has worked best for people in their careers and in their lives. We culled notes and letters we've received from people telling us how they have used our ideas, and how they've experienced positive results. We decided it made sense to share these basic elements of their success with a larger audience, which is you.

All walks and levels of people in all sorts of professions were telling us what made them tick in their careers and their lives. From individuals just entering or reentering the work force, to entrepreneurs at the top of the corporate ladder, we have heard a common beat about what has worked and why. We took it upon ourselves to extract the universal wisdom from their stories, as well as our own firsthand experiences, and present them in a way that will benefit others, too.

Our audiences have represented the same rich, culturally diverse melting pot that is the hallmark of America. Men and women from every ethnic and socioeconomic background have contributed to the insights we have garnered over the years. People from a variety of industries and career paths, the young, the old, the struggling, the challenged, the comfortable, and the confused have influenced our point of view.

What we have tried to do in the following pages is not to give you a set of rules to follow, but to give you some very sound and practical concepts to consider—concepts that have guided a great number of people to find satisfaction in their careers and their lives. Some of what we'll offer will be familiar to you. But we are not attempting to teach you something— we are hoping to go beyond your intellect and impact your life in a very practical way. We want to offer you the tools to improve your daily lives on the job and off the job.

Our insights into career and life issues, however, are only part of the journey we hope to take you on. The other part concerns a journey that you must make on your own—the journey inward to the very crevices of who you are. On the journey to self-discovery, there is always only one traveler, and that is you. Who you are predicates who you'll be, and you can only make the most out of yourself and your life after taking a thorough inventory of who is at the starting gate.

Be prepared to engage your imagination as you venture out on that road to become the best that you can be. Beneath every remarkable human accomplishment is the drive to be better. Each of us can be propelled beyond our own limitations and mediocrity to make our lives stand out like bright stars. Besides honesty, drive, commitment, and tenacity, it takes a willingness carved out of the very heart of who you are.

Stop for a moment now and imagine a marksman's target. Overlay the things that are most important to you on the tar- get—the things you want to accomplish and the fulfillment you want to achieve. Now imagine that you are shooting an arrow at the target. If you hit it right in the center, then you will achieve what you wish to achieve. Imagine the arrow to be all of your effort channeled in the direction of your goals. The arrow is a powerful tool that carries the essence of who you are and where you want to go. If you have no defined goals, no real desires, no objective of fulfillment, then you have no bull's-eye toward which to focus your arrow. The object of this book is to help you to create a target for your life and to help you find ways to channel your energy into the arrow that will hit it.

So buckle up and get ready for the journey. One last word of caution before you begin: Do not confuse who you are with what you do for a living. No job has a mind, soul, or heart—but you do. You are an individual, and that is the basis of your importance to yourself and to the world. A job is only as important as the individual behind it. Without the intelligence, the personality, the creativity, and the individuality that you bring to it, it is nothing at all.

Throughout the book we have provided space for you to write down your thoughts and goals. This is meant to be a "thought book," not a workbook. We do not have the answers to your success and happiness—we recognize with respect that your life is a work in progress. We will not make any guarantees, but we do hope to take you on an enticing exploration that unearths important caverns to who you are, not present you with an arduous task. Our challenge is to get through to you—to confront you with new thoughts (or long-forgotten thoughts) and to give you some important tools to implement the changes you desire in your life.

Welcome aboard and have a great trip!

—Jeri and Rick

PART I

KNOW THYSELF

. . . To thine own self be true,
And it must follow, as the night the day,
Thou canst not then be false to any man.
                                    —*William Shakespeare*

In good times and in bad times, the best preparation for the future is an investment in yourself. After friends and fortunes have come and gone, you—and the ideals you hold dearest to you—will remain.

We invite you to come along on a journey to explore the dreams, the intricacies, and the magic that make you different from anyone else in the world. And in taking the close look at the mosaic of who you are, we implore you to push yourself to the very edges of your own subjective sense of personal excellence. That personal excellence is only attainable by measuring up to the innermost elements that drive you—the very things that constitute your individuality.

The first step on the journey, then, is to discover those things at the very heart of who you are—those things that drive you and shape your dreams. The next step is to find expression for them in your life. The rest is up to you. It is our hope that you can turn the things that lie at the heart of your being into the very foundation on which your life is built and the axis from which it revolves.

Chapter One

What Makes You Tick?

Alas, for those who never sing, but die with all their music in them.

—Oliver Wendell Holmes

As human beings, each of us is made up of flesh, blood, and bones, and we are all driven by basic needs of survival. Beyond our basic needs, however, each of us is driven by our own special set of desires, interests, motivations, and goals—the very things that make us different from anyone else. Some of us are driven by money, some by success, competition, fame, caring for others, some by knowledge, and some are driven by the love of various objects or pastimes. Some of us are driven by unknown fears, while some are driven by a relentless fear of failure. Some people are driven by many things. At the very root of who we are lie the things that are most important to us—the things that make us tick.

In order to find fulfillment as the unique individuals that we are, we must first know what's most important to us—what we value, what excites us, and what keeps us going when things get tough.

When asking yourself what makes you tick, some of you will be able to answer easily, while others may have to think a good, long time to get to those things that define you most. Part of the difficulty is that often the most basic things about us

3

never find a place in our daily lives. We are all moving so quickly that we do not take the time to know ourselves or identify those things that drive us. We often put our needs and desires on the bottom of our life's marquee while various daily requirements receive top billing. In time we begin living our lives by rote—we go to work, have lunch with So-and-So on Tuesday, we do our banking, our shopping, our tending to our households, visiting, lounging, we plan some weekend excursions, and whatever other things that keep the structure of our lives in place. Most of us could put ourselves on automatic pilot and probably not miss out on very much. Society complicates the matter by constantly trying to homogenize our needs and desires by lumping us together into one mass identity. Instead of learning about what is most us, we end up learning about what society wants us to be.

Finding Out What Makes You Tick

If you have become so entrenched in your day-to-day habit of living that you've lost touch with your most basic needs and desires, take a minute now to consider what makes you feel better than anything else—what gives you that excited, happy feeling about being alive. When asking our audiences what makes them tick, their answers fill quite a spectrum: respect, money, recognition, security, material possessions, power, freedom, fun, a balanced life, good friends, family, responsibility, health, and independence.

One of the most popular answers our audiences give is freedom, and we discovered that for many, freedom is expressed through traveling. More often than not, however, traveling represents a ticket out of the not-so-fulfilling daily lives we've created for ourselves rather than an inherent interest. We enjoy traveling because it is an escape from the tedium that has

WHAT MAKES YOU TICK?   5

overtaken our lives—that we have allowed to overtake our lives. How many of us are guilty of working at jobs we hate for the security of a paycheck? Our vacations come and we run away as fast as we can so we can forget for five, ten, or fifteen days (if we're lucky) what it is we have to go back to. We're not traveling to pleasure, we're traveling from pain. If traveling, then, was your answer to what makes you tick and these were the reasons, try again.

You might be saying, "No, I disagree, I really do love to travel, and I don't travel to escape. In fact, I like my job and the rest of my life." For you, then, traveling probably *is* something that makes you tick. But what underlies your love of travel? It's probably an innate love of exploring. Just as Columbus, Vespucci, Lewis and Clark, and other great explorers were driven by their desire to seek out new territory, you, too, were probably born with a thirst to see the world. Since there are no new continents to discover or explore, people with that basic tendency today usually express and satisfy it through travel. And if you were born with the traveling bone and you know it, you're lucky, because it is a trait that does not take kindly to being thwarted.

We met a man from Cleveland, Ohio, who was obsessed with hating where he lived. Practically every other word out of his mouth made some derogatory reference to Cleveland. After years of this kind of talk, he put in for a transfer to another city where his company operated. When a position opened up in Oakland, California, he and his wife and two children made the pilgrimage out West.

Instantly, he was a changed man—he could say nothing wrong about his new city and, in fact, doted on it like a new father. His infatuation continued for about two and a half years until little complaints about Oakland began creeping into his speech. It wasn't long before Oakland, too, was on his enemy list, and he became a disgruntled person all over again. His wife put two and two together and realized a vacation was in order. She booked a trip to Mexico, and before they even got there, her husband was a changed man again—falling in love with life all over. From then on, they planned two trips a year to a place they had never been before or to revisit favorite places. Having discovered his latent traveling bone, our friend even signed up for night school at a community college and began to study world history, which enabled him to travel the world through time in books!

Not everyone is as lucky as our friend from Cleveland. Many of us never do learn what makes us tick and end up spending our lives without receiving any deep satisfaction or joy from anything. We become complacent and accept our lot as if it were assigned by some force outside of us. How do we shake ourselves loose from our dreaded complacency and take charge of our lives and our dreams? What stirred Grandma Moses to start painting at eighty years old? It must begin with a long inward look at the very heart of who we are and, upon seeing what's there, a willingness to change some things in our lives to make the room and the time for the things that will bring us considerable happiness.

Now take a moment to step back and think about why you do some of the things you do. Often the motivation behind the things we do is more revealing than the things themselves. Perhaps you're spinning your wheels doing one thing when you really want to be doing something else. Whatever the case may be, it's your scenario. We can't determine the whys. We only ask that you consider them yourself.

On the Journey

Having already asked yourself what makes you tick puts you ahead of the pack on the journey to discover the answer. It is said that Alice B. Toklas once asked Gertrude Stein, "What's the answer?" and Gertrude responded, "What's the question?" The question is an imperative leg of this journey. You may say to yourself, "I know what makes me tick but there's no way that I can accommodate those things in my life." And to that we say, try and then see what happens.

Let's say one of you has that very concern, and your particular desire (the thing that makes you tick) is to act. You discovered your inclination in high school when you had the lead part in the school play. Your teachers called you a natural, you received standing ovations, and you couldn't fall asleep at night because you were so filled with excitement and anticipation about the next day's performance. Nothing before or since has made you feel the same exhilaration. And although you always said you would study acting one day, other things got in the way and your life proceeded without you pursuing your dream. Now you're a thirty-three-year-old single mother who works fifty hours a week and can barely make ends meet. How in the world are you ever going to find the time or money to include acting in your life?

Well, it certainly won't be easy, but we recommend taking steps to at least get back in touch with your dream. Start by going to the theater from time to time, reading plays, and memorizing monologues. Join a community theater group, and get your children involved if you can. Enjoy your dream vicariously while rekindling your interest. Remember the man from Cleveland who started studying world history in order to travel in his mind? It's the same kind of thing. Our advice to this hypothetical would-be actress is to get as near to her dream to act as she can by immersing herself in the subject. The next step would be to take a drama course at night school. Start, too, going to auditions—you never know what will happen.

Fear of Failing

What we have seen as a big stumbling block that many people run up against in the process of discovery is a fear of failing—a fear that they cannot live up to their dreams. As long as they keep their dreams on a back burner, they feel they are safe—both themselves and their dreams. Not only are they spared the possibility of not measuring up to a long-held ideal, the ideal itself is protected. Often our ideals serve as a sanctuary in our minds and hearts where we can retreat to when we feel unfulfilled in our daily lives or when the world is too much with us. If the would-be actress, for example, finally did go to acting school and found out she wasn't very good at it, she would lose that very special feeling about herself and what her life might have been. Putting our dreams to the test, then, makes us risk losing them if we fail, and no longer can they act as a safe harbor.

But dreams unrealized can become places where we harbor a deep sense of loss and failure, too. The tighter we hold onto our dreams, the smaller they become. Instead of finding sanctuary and preservation, we find unease and inertia. Something eats away at us until we are left with an empty, lost feeling about who we are. The tension between what our lives have become and our imagination of what could have been becomes too sharp to live with comfortably. Regret begins to set in and we spend a good deal of our lives blaming ourselves for setting the trap—for being less than we could have been. So when feeling hemmed in by doubt and fear of failure about pursuing your dreams, try to envision the doubt and failure you're sure to feel if you don't. Remember, too, what one poet said: "Many a desert flower is born to blush unseen and waste its sweetness on the desert air."

Checkpoint

So where are you now? Hopefully, we've helped get you thinking and you've asked yourself some important questions, have come up with some answers, gained insight into who you are and what makes you tick, and perhaps have even come up with some ideas as to how to put some dreams into motion. If you're like most people, you are experiencing some hesitation. Try not to be dismayed. It's a natural feeling that almost always accompanies growth and change. There's something in all of us that resists change. As unrewarding as some parts of our lives may be, they have nonetheless become familiar to us. Familiarity brings comfort, and we all take solace in our daily rituals. That, in fact, is the very reason many people never change.

The best way to get past your hesitation is by replacing one kind of comfort with another. Sacrifice some of the comfort you receive from the very predictability of your life for a new kind of comfort that comes from discovering, exploring, and nurturing new dimensions in yourself. In time these new parts will be familiar to you, too. Not only will your life give you a deeper comfort from its increased meaning and sense of fulfillment, it will give you a sense of security about who you are—that you are the kind of person you can rely on to challenge and meet your dreams.

All this is not to say that change happens overnight. You have to realize that a person spends a good many years becoming who they are. Change, if it is to be lasting, takes time, too. It necessitates a period of self-scrutiny, opening up, creating new habits, new ways to spend one's time, and new expectations.

The time factor itself disheartens many on the journey through self-discovery because we are all so conditioned to expect and want instant results and gratification. From day one we are bombarded with media messages to fix things in a flash—from microwavable fast food to fantastic brands of aspirin to take away our pain. If we want to go to Spain, we hop on a jet and are there in less than eight hours—a journey that at one time took months. So much of our lives is barren of process that we have learned to expect that nothing should take very much time, and when it does, we reflexively try to resist it.

The truth is, however, most important things do require a process and do take time. There's no such thing as a quickie medical school program, and it's a good thing there isn't. There is no bypassing the long years of devotion and care that go into being a good parent, and there is no expert at anything who hasn't spent the time, effort, conscientiousness, and steadfast commitment necessary to acquire expertise in their field.

So be prepared to buck whatever socialization stands in the way of you making your dreams come true or expressing what makes you tick. If what you always wanted to do more than anything else is to grow flowers, then grow flowers. Read the books, buy the seeds, the pots, the soil, make the greenhouse or flower boxes, dig your fingers into the earth, and spend the time needed to become the gardener that you know in your heart you are. There is no, nor should there be, getting around the toil involved in planting and nurturing the very flower that you are in the unique garden that is your life.

Follow the Beat of Your Own Drum

We mentioned early on in the chapter that society often strips us of our own identity by lumping us into one mass identity with similar needs and desires. In the process of such homogenization, society creates a manageable and predictable status quo. Once a status quo is established, society's job is to maintain it. Serving mainly to control and proscribe people's behavior, a status quo generally is a closed system that locks individuals out. The message, however subtle and hidden, is loud and clear: "Don't be an individual. Individuals are too hard to manage and predict."

You may think our thoughts on the subject are a little farfetched. You might be thinking, "This country has always stood behind an individual's freedom of speech and expression. And we, as a society, admire free thinkers." But do we really? Think back to even your earliest days in grammar school. Everyone remembers chiding or having been chided for wearing the wrong clothes or not wanting to play kickball when everyone else was playing the game.

These very first rules about conformity are the rudiments of the status quo. As social animals, ostracism is very painful to us. We go out of our way to blend in with the pack in order to avoid being singled out of the crowd. What ends up happening is that we modify our impulses—perhaps the very things that make us tick—to secure the approval of our peers and family. Conformity, for most of us, is a lifelong habit.

What we must do, as adults, is remind ourselves that we are self-sufficient individuals with the internal resources necessary to be our own agents of approval. We must let our own self-expectations be the measure of our comfort and fulfillment, not someone else's. Just remember that as you journey outside the self-definitions that have been handed to you, there will be a lot of social pressure on you not to listen to your own drummer. People will want you to be just like them and they'll have no qualms or tact about letting you know it. But, remember, if you turn out to be great at what you do differently, everyone will admire you. And even if they don't, the important thing is that you admire yourself for being the person you most want to be. Your life is a one-time event, make sure you write the script.

Final Thoughts

To those of you who have been waiting all your life for a little nudge on the shoulder from behind, this is it. We wrote this book to get you started on a journey of personal excellence that we hope you will continue the rest of your life. It is a journey that begins with who you are now and ends with you being the best that you can be in everything you do. We don't mean the best in any competitive sense, but rather in terms of quality of life.

Unfortunately, many of us lose touch with our most basic selves and inclinations because they were never nurtured or encouraged. We heard a story about a three-year-old girl who created beautiful designs in the dirt with sticks while playing in her front yard. Her parents worked in science professions and held great aspirations for their daughter to become a scientist, too. They discouraged her interest in art and kept trying to build her interest in science. They enrolled her in summer science programs throughout her early school years despite her pleas to enroll in art programs. By the time she was in high school, her interest in art had pretty much been beaten out of her. Instead of developing an interest in science, she grew to resent it and ended up dropping out of college altogether.

No matter what may have happened to your desires up to

this point in the journey of your life, we are convinced that it is never too late to discover or rediscover them. By defining, discovering, and aiming at your own target of excellence—and setting a standard of excellence that is right for you—we are convinced that you will lead a more fulfilling life. Knowing what makes you tick is the very blueprint of your target of personal excellence. Aiming at your target is impossible without knowing what it is or where to find it. Sure, you could aim at anyone's target, but the point of this book is that you aim at your own. We invite you to hitch your sights to your very own star, not someone else's. And when you do take that piercing look into the galaxy of who you are, be prepared—you might just discover a whole constellation.

Notes to Yourself

Here are some questions to assist you in discovering what makes you tick. We ask that as you think about the questions, you also think about yourself in the big picture. Try not to compartmentalize your life into divisions, such as personal versus professional. Concentrate, instead, on the "whole you" by looking at your life in its totality.

- What makes you tick? Write down the things you value most in life. Think in terms of people, places, interests, endeavors, events, and actions.
- What feelings of joy and fulfillment do you derive from each? Describe.
- What excites and challenges you?
- What activities bring out the best in you?
- What would you want to have inscribed on your tombstone?
- What two adjectives best describe you today?
- What two adjectives would you like to best describe you?

- What do you consider to be your greatest accomplishments?
- Do you have positive childhood or past memories of something you used to enjoy doing but no longer do? Describe.
- Is there something in your life that you've done and wish you could do again? Describe.

Do you see common threads or patterns in your answers to these questions? If so, take a moment to think about the relationships you've discovered, perhaps even write down your reflections. And as more answers come to you, add them to your list. Your list is like your life—a work in progress. This process we are inviting you to take is the same one that has helped many people we've interacted with to not only achieve their goals, but to receive a greater sense of overall satisfaction. Remember, the best investment you can make in the '90s is in yourself!

Chapter Two

Back to Basics: Believing in Yourself

Believe in yourself! Have faith in your abilities! Without a humble but reasonable confidence in your own powers you cannot be successful or happy.

—*Norman Vincent Peale*

Having taken a close look at the things that make you tick, how do you get to the point where your life *is* what makes you tick? There's only one sure starting point—BELIEVING IN YOUR-SELF. You are the one person who can make it happen! You are the one person who can believe that what you want is possible! Walking through the door to believe in ourselves—that magically liberating force in each of us—is like walking into an infinitely limitless sky where there are no boundaries. Our journey now is to look at the stars that fill that sky.

How many times have you wanted to do something but talked yourself out of it before you even started? How many times have you started a project and stopped? How many times have you said to yourself, "I can't." Have you ever stopped to look behind the "can't"? If not, do it now. Think back and try to remember that feeling—a time you wanted something but didn't believe in yourself enough to go after it. What got in the way—what kept you from believing in yourself?

Where It All Begins

Our worth as individuals is something we are born having in common with everyone else. How that original worth grows influences how we come to believe in ourselves. The people, endeavors, pastimes, and actions that fill our lives either nurture or hurt our feelings of worth.

Our worth begins to grow by being given unconditional approval and acceptance for who we are. Our initial feelings of worth are built upon by our parents acknowledging, approving, and encouraging our first accomplishments—whether we are reaching for a rattle or holding our heads up on our own. From our parents' reassuring recognition, feelings of worth begin to blossom into feelings of confidence and we begin to believe in who we are and what we can do.

A Seed Is Planted

Two friends of ours who live in California had their first child, Seth, in their early thirties. One of Seth's earliest fascinations was airplanes. When he saw them for the first time in picture books, his eyes shone so brightly that the whole room lit up. From then on, every toy, blanket, T-shirt, and bed sheet involved airplanes, and Seth loved every single one of them. When he was old enough to speak, he asked questions about them; when he was old enough to put Legos together, he created facsimiles of them; when he learned how to draw, he drew them; and, needless to say, when he was old enough to put models together, he and his parents manufactured whole plastic fleets of them.

The message to Seth from his parents was that he was worthwhile and the interests he had were worthwhile, as well. His parents' unconditional approval, acceptance, and encouragement of who Seth was provided him with a strong message of his worth and eventual belief in himself. It's not surprising that Seth wants to be a pilot when he grows up—and it will be surprising if he doesn't!

You, Your Own Gardener

We told Seth's story at a seminar we delivered in Seattle, Washington, and it evoked almost an opposite story from Tom, a veterinarian from Vancouver. No matter what Tom had done while growing up, it was never good enough for his father. If Tom played baseball, his father would say football was better; if he bagged groceries after school, his father would say he should mow lawns; if he got B's on his report card, his father criticized him for not being able to get A's. His father even found fault with the girls Tom took out on dates.

From all the negative messages Tom received about his choices, Tom's self-confidence was pretty precarious. But something in him kept fending his father's messages off. He managed to listen to his own voice—the one he created from his own experiences—being a good ballplayer, his after-school jobs, and his above-average performance in school. All the things he did made him believe in himself, despite his father's attempts to undermine his worth.

When Tom was thirteen, he got a summer job in a veterinarian's office. Tom loved animals and he was inspired by watching the vet in action. He decided he wanted to be a veterinarian, too. His dream to be a vet grew year after year, and when it came time to apply to college, he chose one that had the best preveterinarian program. His father, naturally, disapproved. As much as Tom would have wanted his father's support and admiration, he had learned to live without it. Tom succeeded in becoming a veterinarian and, to this day, his father calls him a "dog doctor," implying that he wasn't good enough to be a "real" doctor.

The important thing about Tom's story is that it shows the strength of our own voice in our self-worth. He overcame a very early obstacle to his self-worth, and was able to create it on his own. He learned to be his own source of approval and acceptance.

We Are Not What We Do

If love and approval are given *conditionally* from day one—and we do not become our own source of approval, as Tom did—our feelings of worth become contingent upon what we do, not who we are. If we don't perform in a certain way, we do not feel important or worthwhile as individuals. The message is very destructive because it teaches us that it's what we do and not who we are that is important.

How many of you have felt devastated by losing a job, as if that job had more to do with who you are than you yourself? A job is external to us and, like any external thing, should never define us. We all fall prey to the danger of defining ourselves by the things we do. The very language we use is set up to make us do so by relying so heavily on titles—doctor, speech therapist, writer, mother, father, and so on. How many of us have asked people what they do for a living and had them respond, "I'm a communications specialist," or "I'm a human resources executive," or "I'm a writer"? Those answers make it sound as though they have become the thing they do.

Wouldn't it be interesting if we described the things we do for a living or as pastimes with verbs instead of nouns: "I write," "I practice medicine," "I teach children." By using verbs to describe what we do, we keep our lives in a truer perspective. We do not become our jobs, we are people who have jobs and perform specific tasks while we do them. Verbs make it sound as if there's a human being doing the thing involved in a particular job or pastime. Titles make it sound as if you *are* the thing or things that you do.

Matters of Confidence

Confidence shall be your strength.

—*Isaiah 30:15*

Our feelings of worth lay the groundwork for our self-confidence. Ideally, we learn to trust in our ability to do things, which gives us the confidence to try other things. Success at each new thing we do inspires yet another new endeavor. The whole process spirals so that we experience an ever-increasing level of confidence throughout our lives.

The problem, however, is that it rarely is so simple. If it were, we wouldn't constantly sell ourselves short, stay in jobs or personal relationships that don't challenge our growth, or ever lead unfulfilling lives. Too often people learn to feel limited. We are not psychologists and we won't delve into how people learn to harbor diminished expectations of themselves. As practitioners, however, we will look at confidence through the experiences of the people we've met or heard about through our work.

Confidence Hang-ups

While giving a speech at a conference in Atlanta last year, we heard a story about a man who had a gift for restoring old cars. He was a fix-it man by trade and would often accept old cars as payment for jobs he would perform. He would take these old cars (Thunderbirds, 1957 Chevys, Datsun 240Zs, etc.)— that were most often ready for the junk heap—and restore them to their original condition. When he was finished with one of his masterpieces, he'd usually trade it for a couple more old clunkers and start the whole process over again.

It was obvious to us that this man was driven by restoring old cars—not only the body work, but mechanical work as well. Restoring cars, then, was what made him tick. The story about him came up in a casual conversation about cars during a coffee break. A colleague just happened to mention that he had purchased a fully restored 1972 Datsun 240ZX for $1,200, a classic car with a market value of anywhere from $7,000 to $12,000. When we asked why he was able to buy the car for so little, he said, "Because the guy had no self-confidence."

After asking a few more questions, we learned that the man made $5 an hour as a general handyman and did all of his work on cars for fun. Although he could have had a job in any car detailing shop—or his own shop—his lack of belief in himself and his ability prevented him from putting himself out into the world. Not only was he depriving himself of a much better livelihood, he was keeping himself from making a living at what he did best and loved most.

Where Is Your Hidden Giant?

With sound self-confidence you can succeed.
—*Norman Vincent Peale*

Low self-confidence is most often expressed in much less exaggerated ways. A closet chef, for example, might feel more comfortable going out to dinner at a gourmet restaurant than he or she would trying to prepare a gourmet meal. Low self-confidence convinces such a person not to put their dream to the test. A person who has a dream of making beautiful clothes, but has no self-confidence, is likely to spend a fortune on an elaborate wardrobe instead of attempting to create a pattern for one of his or her designs. And the would-be writer may spend all his or her free time reading great books instead of writing one. Where do you hide your giant?

The Myth of Confidence

The myth of self-confidence is thinking that it is something that you are born having or not having. It's not. Often when we describe someone, we speak in terms of he or she being a self-confident person or a person who has no self-confidence, as if self-confidence were a personality attribute. The truth is that it is something we learn. Many things happen that affect a person's confidence—good and bad—so that it is in constant need of alignment. Any failure can set back a person with a lot of self-confidence, and a success can greatly increase the confidence of someone who has low self-confidence.

We met a person, Steve, who we thought was the most self-confident person in the world. He was thirty-two years old and president of a large accounting firm. Having spent an entire evening with him at a dinner party hosted by a mutual friend, we heard his life story, which turned out to be one tale of success after another. Everything Steve did, he did well. When we asked him what his secret was, he said, "I guess I just never thought there was anything I couldn't do."

Three years later we asked our friend who had hosted that dinner how our accountant acquaintance was doing. She told us that in a desperate attempt to battle the recession, Steve's company had reorganized and left him and many other executives out of the reorganization plan. Having never (as far as we know) experienced anything but success and upward movement, Steve was devastated. Instead of picking himself up and putting himself back into the job market, he spent six months trying to figure out what he had done wrong. He was so accustomed to succeeding that anything but success paralyzed him. He took the whole thing much too personally because he had allowed too much of his self-definition to be tied up in feeling successful.

The truth, was that his company's reorganization was no reflection upon him at all—it was simply a tactic many companies resort to in an attempt to appease nervous shareholders in a bad economy. Executives at the helm are typically treated like modern-day corporate scapegoats and sacrificed. In Steve's case a little taste of failure along the way would have better prepared him for his bitter, unexpected change in fortune.

Crisis and Confidence

That which does not kill us makes us stronger.
—Friedrich Nietzsche

Contrary to our initial expectations, personal or professional crisis has the potential not only to make us stronger, but also to set us off into new directions that can inspire our confidence. In *The Confidence Factor* (MasterMedia, 1990), Judith Briles reports that 90 percent of the highly successful women she surveyed said they experienced some form of personal or professional crisis—divorce, death, tragic accident, being fired, losing money, bankruptcy—and all said that it made them better at what they were currently doing. Her findings echo Chinese wisdom, which views crisis as opportunity—a time to look around, take stock of our lives with heightened intensity, and aim our sights at something that will ground us and help us grow.

Think Positive!

Keeping a positive mental attitude is very important to confidence and believing in yourself. Positive thoughts are the beginnings of positive actions. It is not always enough for you, yourself, to think positive, but you ought to surround yourself with others who do, too. Judith Briles says in *The Confidence Factor* that being around negative people is a major factor in having low confidence. "Negative thinking, negative energy, is like a sponge. It absorbs and consumes just about anything around it." One of the "Accomplished Women" she interviewed said, "I'm a real believer in affirmations. I buy tapes. I buy books. I tune out anyone negative, only listen to the positive."

If you can't get away from negativity entirely, work on your ability to tune it out or combat it with your own positivity. The same thing goes for negative mental tapes—the negative voices that you may have heard in your life. Remember our veterinarian friend, Tom? Not only was he able to tune out his father's persistent negativism, he was able to tape over it with his own positive voice.

Getting Beyond Negativity

You also have to try to convert negative experiences into positive ones. In her book, Briles cites many examples of how highly successful women have turned negatives into positives: "When brokerage vice president Susan Kingsolver found herself derailed on the fast track, she was finally able to use it as an opportunity and move on. 'After wasting a lot of time bemoaning the situation, I decided to take it as positive. I had been presented with an opportunity to reassess a lot of things in my life and move forward.' "

While giving a talk on goals in New York City recently, the discussion began to get stuck on everyone's "can'ts." Most of the "can't do" thinking sprang from various old mental tapes that people were carrying around telling them that they needed to do more. "My father's expectations of me were much too stringent. . . . To this day, I hear him saying, 'No, you're not doing it right!' Or, simply, "You're not good enough!" Finally, a man in the group said, "Let's just get on with it! That was then, this is now! Why waste this time talking about what we can't do?!" The force and timing of his comment was oddly liberating, and instead of resistance, it evoked a shift to a "can do" direction.

Stepping Stones

Accomplishing goals—however big or small—in your personal or professional life is a stepping stone to self-confidence. Keep track of your victories, and don't look at your defeats under a microscope! Turn whatever blows you receive into inspiration to do better; don't be knocked down!

Start with simple goals. Accomplishing a task successfully gives birth to a feeling of confidence, which sets you up for the next goal. The self-confidence you feel will inspire you to more competent actions which, in turn, increases your confidence—like a chain reaction. The same is true for low confidence. If you never challenge yourself to try new things or increase your competence at something, you perpetuate a lack of confidence. At some point you have to put yourself on the line!

The Importance of Taking Risks

Another myth that often shrouds how we think about self-confidence is that it requires an original level of competence. That's an absurd notion when you stop to think about it, because it implies that we're born competent at something. We may be born with inclinations for something, such as art, music, literature, mathematics, or airplanes, but we only gain competence through repeated exposure, study, and practice.

One of the most important ingredients that go into developing self-confidence is the willingness to take risks to do something without knowing what the outcome will be. It also requires a willingness to accept the possibility that you might fail. The idea of failure is paralyzing to many people. The very thought of it keeps them from trying to do the thing or things they want most to do.

The big fear of failure ends up, ironically, creating failure. If you don't test your dreams or try to do something that's important to you, you fail. However passive the failure is, it is failure nonetheless. That's why it's so important to allow room for failure in how you view success. If failure—a form of crisis—can be looked at as a possible source of strength and life expansion, the thought of it wouldn't inhibit us so much.

Not Me!

We've met many people over the years who have said, "Not me, I could never do that." We've heard the same phrase used to describe ambitions in careers, business, personal relationships, sports, and even hobbies. These same people usually proceed to cite examples of other people who do the very same thing they want to do perfectly. They forget, however, that those same people they cite in their examples had to have taken risks several times—and probably even failed several times—to attain their levels of competence. Success rarely happens on the first go-round—repetition was probably the real mother of invention.

Self-confidence also requires a willingness to leave your

comfort zone and enter uncharted territories. If you never go beyond what you know, how can you ever know more? Accomplishments have the potential to bring joy into our lives. They allow us to see ourselves grow, to have a sense of attaining something that's important to us, and to give us the confidence to keep dreaming and even attain the dreams we dream. If we keep ourselves in exile within our self-made prisons, our worlds will never extend beyond those narrow walls.

Believe in Yourself!

Belief in one's self is what naturally grows out of a well-nurtured sense of worth and self-confidence. It's a pleasant blend of the two, and has an ongoing quality about it. Believing in ourselves is the overriding feeling we have while doing the daily things that make up our lives. It is really how we approach life. We can feel confident about certain endeavors, but we believe in ourselves as human beings who have a rightful and important place in the world.

We mentioned the story of a man who had a gift for restoring old cars, but did not make it his livelihood because he had no self-confidence. We want to take a minute to clarify. This really wasn't the best example of low self-confidence, but it was an excellent example about lack of belief in oneself. If this particular person truly suffered from low self-confidence, he probably would never have lived up to his dream to restore old cars in the first place. The fact that he did pursue his dream indicates self-confidence was at work.

What wasn't at work, however, was belief in himself or his ability, which is why he sold the 1972 Datsun 240ZX for $1,200 instead of $8,000. Let's imagine for a moment what he might have felt had he sold it for $8,000. Do you think that receiving the higher price would have raised his belief in himself? We think it would have, because the higher price is symbolic, and would have made him feel differently about himself. By asking more and receiving the higher price, his old perception of himself would be challenged. That's not to say that we think he would be a changed man overnight, but we do think it might trigger the beginning of a change in his feelings of belief in himself. Self-perceptions take a long time to become established and change occurs gradually.

Be Your Own Hero

We met a financial analyst who told us that as a little girl, she believed in everything from the sandman to Santa Claus. As she grew up to discover that her childhood heroes were fantasies, she took her wonderful capacity to believe in something and applied it to real people in her life—her mother, certain teachers and professors, and various other shining stars that crossed her path.

When struggling to mount the stairway of her dream to become one of the five top analysts at her company, she decided to make herself her hero. She recounted daily every success she had ever had, looked at every obstacle she ever hurdled, remembered how hard she had worked for everything she had ever wanted, and told herself over and over, "If anyone can do it, I can!" Today she is a top analyst on Wall Street.

Valuing Your Life

A good way to challenge belief in yourself is to stop and consider how important you and your life really are. Have you ever imagined what other people's lives would be like without you? Think about it. . . . What would your parents' lives, your brothers' and sisters' lives, your spouse's life, and your children's lives be like without your presence? The moment we're born we begin to impact the lives of others—a process that continues throughout our lives.

We all remember the story of George Bailey, played by Jimmy Stewart in *It's a Wonderful Life*. On the brink of despair, George attempts to end his life but is saved by his own personal angel, Clarence. Clarence takes George on a journey back in time to show him what an important difference his life has made in so many other lives, as well as in the fate of his community, Bedford Falls. Deeply moved by what he sees, George is filled with a tremendous sense of the value of his life, and begins to believe in himself once again.

Although our own scenarios may not be quite as dramatic as George Bailey's, we may each find just how wonderful we and our lives are if we look closely enough. And although probably none of us will be as lucky as George to be granted our own personal angel, we can be our own angels—the very ones who sit on our shoulders at all times, telling us we matter, that we count, that we make a difference! That is what believing in ourselves really is! Let the angel you are to yourself be the voice that reminds you of the contributions you have made, the kindness you have bestowed, and of the very vital sparks that you alone have put into the world. And with that very precious knowledge, believe in who you are.

Final Thoughts

So much of this chapter has been about what's at work in us that helps us to believe in ourselves. Self-worth, self-confidence, and believing in ourselves are so cross-pollinated that it's hard to talk about one without evoking another. Each combines to give us a feeling of the abundant possibilities that are available to us. In the end no force but ourselves will stop us from attaining what we want. If we put up barriers along the way, we have to tear them down. If failure meets us, we have to turn it into opportunity. If we don't try, we only have ourselves to blame. Believe in yourself! Throw yourself into the sky, like a kite, and stretch out into the horizons of your dreams!

Chapter Three

Create Your Own Definition of Success

There is only one success—to be able to spend your life in your own way.

—*Christopher Morley*

Definitions of success are tied into our very first perceptions of the values of the world. And, unfortunately, success in our society is linked primarily to material status—how much money you make, what professional rank or title you possess, and the things you own that are a reflection of your status. Although there have been brief moments in this country's history when we have reached for a broader, more subjective definition of success—thanks mainly to the Utopian movements of the nineteenth century, Ralph Waldo Emerson and Henry David Thoreau, the Great Depression, and the 1960s and early '70s—no movement was ever sustained long enough to influence a permanent change in our thinking.

Adieu to the '80s

The 1980s brought a new charge to our long-held perceptions of success. In fact success was the buzzword of that decade as practically everyone aspired to having big jobs, big money, and many material things. As Zig Ziglar, a motivational speaker, said, "Everyone was listening to the same radio station—WIIFM—what's in it for me." And life was lived that way. Some people achieved their goals and thought that they would live happily ever after, while others sought high goals with an unwavering focus without ever attaining them.

Life probably would have kept on that way had the bottom not fallen out of the economy and caused the reality of the '80s to shatter. And although some people are still mesmerized by that mind-set, many of us have stopped to rethink our life paths, as well as what it means to be successful. Success, we are beginning to notice, has got to be more lasting, something more sustainable—something more dependable and less changeable.

Enter the '90s

While the '80s held forth the promise of economic prosperity, the '90s, we think, will offer a different kind of prosperity—a kind of personal prosperity that is much more concerned with a happiness that transcends external boundaries. Bill Clinton, who won the presidency in an electoral landslide, seems to embody the new thinking as he speaks of the '90s as the time when we must look at harder truths and moral principles. Success for the '90s will have less to do with the traditional benchmarks of money, power, and feelings of superiority, and more to do with the worth, values, and happiness one feels as an individual.

Success, if it is to be lasting and accessible to all, has to be redefined as a feeling—a state of mind. Success is feeling joy and harmony in living. These feelings come from within us and are the true riches of the mind and soul. The best possible definition of success, we think, is a feeling of personal fulfill-

ment with who you are and the achievements that are important to you.

Growing up, many of us were taught to aim for the highest
and come down a little if necessary. We were told to study hard
so that we could get into a good college, which, in turn, would
lead to a great job. That great job would be the means by which
we would make our fortunes, and that, in turn, would earn us
our highest laurel—success in the eyes of others. We haven't
heard of many instances where parents have told their children
to strive for happiness and personal fulfillment. Happiness, we
are told, comes as a consequence of fulfilling those first requirements—if at all.

The Stuff from Which Success Is Made

In looking at success as the experience of joy in who you are
and the things you do, we also want to note the importance of
having a sense of accomplishment. Accomplishments, like success, come in all shapes and sizes. Again, it's up to you. And
monetary security may very well be a result of doing what you
enjoy doing. The afternoon talk shows have been full of people
who got off the fast track and gave up the six-figure salaries to
have the time and kinds of lives that made more sense to them.
The "Is this all there is?" sensibility brought many people away
from the pursuit of things and to new paths that would lead
them to satisfying their quieter, deeper needs.

We don't mean to sound as though we are against monetary
security, or that it does not in some way contribute to a person's overall feeling of success. What we want to stress is that
monetary security should not be viewed as the be-all and
end-all of feeling successful. It can, indeed, play a part, or for
some, it may not play a part at all. What's most important in

success is that it be considered your own recipe, and that you are the chef who determines the ingredients that go into it.

Often people perceive success as an object and spend their lives aiming at it. They see success as something at "the end of the line" and they wear blinders in pursuing it. The problem is that they often miss out on the myriad things worth seeing—worth knowing—in the periphery. Success, we truly feel, is a journey, not a destination. For on that journey of what our lives are we come in touch with the thousand things that constitute us—the experiences, the feelings, the understandings, the conflicts, the angst, the mercies, the triumphs, the loss, the strengths, and the frailties. And out of all those things, we discover what's most important to us—what we love, what makes our lives worth living. And it's in that very process of discovery that we discover what success is to us, and to us alone.

It stands to reason, then, that success can never be defined from the outset. Success, like our lives, comes out of a process. That's why, too, it should not be handed to us as something that exists outside of us. Like anything else that really counts, success is a subjective event. No one can determine what success should be for us any more than someone can determine what's important to us. It is something that only our feelings can decide.

The Myth of Money

Often we hear of people who have monetary and material wealth committing suicide, having family problems or drug and alcohol problems. Many wealthy people are unable to have meaningful relationships in their lives. Yes, they may have money and material possessions, but not all wealthy people lead successful lives. Edwin Arlington Robinson's poem "Rich-

ard Cory" expresses poignantly the idea that monetary success
does not always translate into personal success:

> Whenever Richard Cory went down town,
> We people on the pavement looked at him:
> He was a gentleman from sole to crown,
> Clean favored and imperially slim.
>
> And he was always quietly arrayed,
> And he was always human when he talked;
> But still he fluttered pulses when he said,
> "Good morning," and he glittered when he
>   walked.
>
> And he was rich—yes, richer than a king—
> And admirably schooled in every grace:
> In fine, we thought that he was everything
> To make us wish that we were in his place.
>
> So on we worked, and waited for the light,
> And went without the meat, and cursed the bread;
> And Richard Cory, one calm summer night,
> Went home and put a bullet through his head.

We met an older, well-to-do woman in San Francisco who had
this to say on the subject of money and success: "It's not money
that's the problem, it's people—they forget that money is only
a means, not an end. If they had a broader, more centered
understanding about what is really important in life, they
wouldn't let money create so many problems for them. I don't
think we should condemn money, but rather condemn a lack
of understanding in people."

During a program we hosted in New York City recently, a
man came up to us after everyone had left the room and said,
"I know what you meant by defining success. To a lot of

people, I was successful. I had made several million dollars, had a beautiful apartment, a weekend house in Connecticut, fancy cars, dined at the best restaurants, and wore the best clothes. I got married and had two children. It sounds very successful, doesn't it? Yet every morning I woke up in pain. I woke up with the fear that I'd lose everything that made everyone think that I was successful. The tragedy was that I didn't even like or need all those things. I would go out and buy a new car and drive it home. I should have been proud, yet as soon as I would get it home, I'd start worrying about what I should do next to keep up the definition of success that others had set for me.

"Then my worst fears started to come true when my business began to falter. Slowly but surely, all my fancy possessions began to disappear and my way of life began to change. I lost a lot of friends—I guess they were worried that the problems I was having might be contagious. A few of my closest, long-standing friends stood by me. I started to get closer to them than I had been in years, and the closer we became, the better I felt. It took me a long time to realize how important they really were to me because I had let my life fall so out of balance.

"What I had rediscovered was that my real success was in having close friends, my family, and sharing my life with other people. It wasn't the cars, the house, the apartment, the travel—they were just excuses for the core elements that were missing in my life. I depended on all those external things to enhance my life, give me an identity. Now it is my family, friends, and who I am as a person that give me my identity and make me feel successful and worthwhile in the world. I'm working at building my professional life back, but not at the expense of the people who are dearest to me. I was lucky to discover what I discovered before it was too late."

It was sad for us to hear about this man's pain. But clearly his story is a success story because he discovered himself, as well as what makes him happy. There is an important lesson in this success story: the importance of failing. We learn more from our failures than we do our achievements, because failure helps us to define what is important to us—what we truly value and want most to achieve. Although failure is painful, the health club adage bears true: "No pain, no gain."

Turning Straw into Gold

Everyone can turn failure into an opportunity. We met a manager of a telemarketing company who taught telemarketers how to sell products over the phone. She would tell her staff that for each ten people they'd call, one would buy the product. She said, "Don't think of 'no' as a rejection, think of it as being one step closer to 'yes.' "

Failure, too, can help you to analyze what went wrong. It can be used to tell you that you're on the right track but you're driving the wrong vehicle. You might be spending all your time in the kitchen washing dishes when you should be cooking fabulous meals! Or perhaps you pour yourself into editing manuscripts while ignoring your talent for writing them. Failure helps a person find his or her place in the world through a process of elimination. "I'm rotten at this, so I'll try that and, lo and behold, I'm a natural." It might not happen on two swings of the bat, but if you stay with it, something very fitting may unveil itself to you.

We're not suggesting that you become a quick quitter—that you give up on something too easily or too early in the game. Thomas Edison created more than ten thousand light bulbs before he turned on the right one, and we'd all be in the dark if he had given up. Walt Disney went bankrupt four times before he succeeded at his dream to create a world of fantastic pleasure and imagination in Disneyland.

The Perils of Perfectionism

For those of you who define success through being a perfectionist, be careful. We have met many perfectionists and reformed perfectionists in our audiences and have found that they continually find themselves up against brick walls. Because they rarely are able to meet or live up to their own standards of perfection, they constantly miss out on feelings of satisfaction and achievement. Their criteria for success are far too steep and, as a consequence, they constantly set themselves up to feel disappointed and inadequate. Too, they miss out on many chances to advance themselves in life and in their careers, because they get so hung up on trying to do things perfectly. It is said that Einstein scored very poorly on an IQ test because he wasn't able to finish it. Why? Because he spent too much time on giving perfect answers to the questions he *did* complete.

Keeping Inner-Focused

Being more inner-focused in our interpretations of success make feelings of success more accessible. Once we learn to be more generous about how we perceive ourselves as successful, we become increasingly available to successes in our lives. Personal success can blossom into a powerful force in our lives. It can because it nurtures our ability to see success in many aspects of our lives. Once we have relaxed our definitions of success, we are freer and more open to see it in places we've never seen it before.

Success can be found in your sense of yourself as being a

person who can love and care for people well, in having important understandings of the world, in seeing yourself as a decent
human being who treats others with respect and dignity, as an
individual who has knowledge of a particular subject or field,
or in the feeling that you are good at what you do for a living.
However you define success, it is an intimately personal affair.
It depends on your values, your interests, your efforts, your
imagination, and your life experiences.

Success as a Quality-of-Life Issue

The good feeling we have about ourselves via the various
successes we perceive increases the meaning and sense of
fulfillment we have about our lives. In this way success is very
much a quality-of-life issue. Only you know what success
means to you, and only you can determine how generous
you'll be in allowing yourself to feel successful. For some of us,
just making it through a day can be viewed as a success!
Whatever the case may be, relish the feeling of success, enjoy
it, and be creative in your measurements of it. We are in this
world for the briefest speck of time, and in the end, the quality
of our lives is the only real, worthwhile standard by which to
judge how successful our lives have been. Unlike the Pharaohs,
we certainly don't take any material thing with us when we go!

The Elusive Secret to Success

How many times have you heard someone ask someone,
"What is the secret to your success?" The question has most
frequently been asked of those who have hit it big in business
and made a lot of money. Money was, and still is for many, the
big green sign of success. Go to any bookstore and see one
get-rich-quick and the-secret-to-my-success title after another.
People always think that there's some elusive secret to success,

some known-by-few password. Hopefully, that myth will be shattered as more and more people stop looking outside themselves to find out what success is all about or how to attain it.

Less frequent is the remark, "You are so successful—you're balancing a family and career, and you and your spouse seem so happy! How do you do it?" Though less frequent than traditional inquiries about success, people are starting to ask this new breed of question.

After a rather intensive seminar we hosted in Chicago last year, a male executive said, "I know what success feels like— it feels like I feel right now! I made it through this session, and I really did learn something important about myself." We bring this up because it is valuable to think of success in terms of specific, discrete accomplishments or feelings. Often there's a temptation to view it as some far-off goal that is only attainable after a given amount of time and effort. The truth is, you can feel success many times and in many different ways about all kinds of things.

Our research on success has revealed that a common element in defining success is movement—we all seek some sort of movement in our lives and in what we do. Most all of us derive satisfaction when we feel that we are making progress and not growing stagnant. We've all heard people complain about their boring lives or their boring jobs. What they are really voicing concern about is the feeling that they are standing still—doing the same thing over and over again without any feeling of growth, challenge, or change. The kind of movement that we equate with success does not necessarily mean we want to climb mountains or acquire vast fortunes, but it does imply that we desire growth—which, not surprisingly, is a fundamental human need. Without growth in our lives, we feel that we are eroding—a feeling that does not promote a sense of success.

Where Are You?

You'll know when you are on the right track to attaining what you identify as success, because you'll have a feeling of happiness. And when you have that feeling, you'll no longer be looking for success, you'll be living it. In the movie *City Slickers,* Billy Crystal played a character who is disenchanted with his fast-paced city life, which is filled with the typical displays of success—a good job, nice home, vacations to Europe. Still, he feels an emptiness about his life and is not happy. Sensing his disenchantment, his wife says to him, "Go find your smile." His smile, of course, is a metaphor for his happiness—a real feeling of success.

When we ask people to start thinking of their definitions of success, we point out how important it is to have something of your very own to shoot for. When something is your own, it necessarily has more meaning and value than something that is determined by someone or something outside you. It also gives you a feeling that you have invested some part of yourself in the very thing you're aiming for. Feelings of ownership and investment in something make you feel more committed to it.

Another thing that is important to keep in mind when defining what success means to you is that it rarely comes from one thing. People often fall into the trap of thinking that only one thing can make them happy, which leads inevitably to disappointment. "Once I get promoted, I'm going to be happy." "Once I get married, I'm going to be happy." "Once I'm finished writing this book, I'm going to be a success." Not only does this approach turn success and happiness into an object, it also keeps it out of reach by putting it in the future. People who do this are continually preparing for their happiness and success, not living it. When the elusive day ever does come, if it does, they wouldn't know happiness if it came up and rubbed across their legs.

Be Your Own Agent of Success

Women constantly are falling prey to this one-day-I'll-be-happy syndrome, since it is a theme that many of them grew up with. "As soon as my prince arrives . . . ." The truth is, he might not! You have got to create your own success. Be a complete person before you let anyone else in. Besides, if you let someone else be responsible for your success, whose success is it? Someone can help you define your dreams and even play a big part in your dreams coming true, but no one can give you what you can't give to yourself. If you have to break out of the cocoon of the kind of thinking that limits the way you look at success, then break out! In determining what success means to you, you have to provide your own internal resources to create the definition that feels best and makes the most sense to you.

As you think about success, think, too, about some of your past hunches about it—instincts that you perhaps squelched for some reason or another. Get back in touch with your gut feelings, examine yourself. And in the examination, if you stumble upon some lost part of yourself—some part that once said, "If I grow up and have a family that I love and that loves me, I will have everything I want"—resurrect it! Listen to that voice and remember each pure and simple measure of success that you ever imagined. That's not to say you have not or cannot add to that measure, you can. What's important to remember is that at some time each of us was very much in tune with what it was to feel joy purely and simply—try to get back to that place.

A friend of ours who works in management at AT&T asked, "Am I thinking too small if I say I want a job that makes me relatively happy? A wife and kids and two vacations a year?" Our answer: Absolutely not! There is no such thing as thinking too small or too big. If you think it, and it feels right to you, it's right! That's exactly what we mean by defining success. You must have your own definition of success and not let anyone tell you what you should or should not strive for.

The Job Hat and Success

For many of us, our jobs are a source of many of our feelings of success. That's because success is readily connected to achievement and our jobs are the most likely environment in which we achieve. There's nothing wrong with deriving feelings of success from your achievements, but do be wary of the temptation to look for all your definitions of success in a job. In today's highly competitive market and terrible economy, companies are laying off workers right and left. If we have too much of our definition of success tied up in what we do at work, then we risk losing more than a job if the time comes when we are let go.

A lot of people who used to think of themselves as having careers now think in terms of having a job. A company's commitment to the employee has diminished and, as a result, job security and the old notion of having a job from the "womb to the tomb" have disappeared. We need to keep a reserve tank so we can still feel good about ourselves and our lives if we lose our jobs. A job, just like money or any external thing, can be taken away from us; success, we have been saying from the beginning, should derive first from the things that are much more intrinsic and permanent.

Final Thoughts

We hope that by the time you get to these last pages, you will feel more in charge of your destiny than you ever have before. By being in control of your own definitions of success, you become the deciding force behind what makes you a successful person. Our hope is that in the process of discovering what success means, you allow yourself to find it in many aspects of who you are—the kind of person you are, your relationships with others, your accomplishments, your sensibilities, your interests, your dreams and ambitions, your past endeavors, and every good thing about you that makes you the individual that you are.

Try to make sure that your equation for success includes what we call some of the softer desires—the qualitative factors—such as what a rose looks like on a Sunday afternoon, a pleasant daydream, a kindness to a stranger, or the color of the sky between day and night. Hone and tailor your definition so that it can fit on the back of a business card. On those days when you can barely keep your head above water, pull out your definition, look at it, take a breath, and smile. Above all, never lose sight of who you are. Success, if it is to mean anything at all, has to be intimately connected to who you are. The success you feel for being the individual that you are should always mean more than any one of many things that you attain in this world.

We don't want you to think that there is no room for material wealth in our approach to defining success. Monetary security may play a part in many people's definition of success since it does provide a means to independence and physical comfort. There's nothing wrong with that. What we are trying to stress is to not let material wealth, nor any other one thing, dominate your perception of success. There are too many folds to who we are and how our lives are put together to ever define ourselves or what it means to be successful by any one element. It just isn't realistic, nor does it serve justice to the many threads in the fabric of who we are. If we can strive to take something from each of the components of our lives when concocting our definition of success, we should come up with a nourishing and satisfying blend that will keep us from the monotony of relying on any one source for our happiness or well-being.

Chapter Four

Setting Your Life Goals

The goal stands up, the keeper
Stands up to keep the goal.

—A. E. Housman

Americans have an unrelenting preoccupation with setting goals. And although we have become experts at setting them, we have much to learn about reaching them. Throughout our talks and travels, we have come across a unique breed of people who are particularly gifted at reaching goals, and we decided to make them—and what works for them—the spotlight of this chapter.

Of all the people we've met, these "goal getters" are by far the most fulfilled in their careers and their lives. They all have created a road map to where they want to go, have figured out how to get there, and know exactly what they want to experience. The qualities that most of the goal getters have in common are passion for their goals, drive and motivation, a sense of direction, discipline, commitment and perseverance, flexibility, an ability to focus themselves, as well as an ability to not set their sights too high.

The Importance of Passion

The first rule to getting anything is wanting it. We are convinced that if you want something enough, you'll figure out a way to get it. The problem for a lot of people in reaching their goals is a failure in desire—they simply don't want it enough. So, how do you conjure up the necessary desire, the passion, to ensure going after something? The truth is, you're probably going after the wrong thing. If you really wanted it, you would have the passion for it. It's hard, if not impossible, to manufacture a desire for something you don't really want. In fact, a lack of desire for a particular pursuit is a built-in protective mechanism to keep you from spending any of your precious life's time on something that you *don't* really want. Your problem isn't that you can't reach your goal, but that you haven't found the right goal. Guaranteed, there's something out there that you do feel passion about, you just have to keep searching.

One of the goal getters whose path we crossed said she was terrible at reaching other people's goals, but great at reaching her own—once she discovered what it was. "I tried just about everything—jogging, cycling, aerobics, walking a mile a day, going after promotions at work, doing all my housework on Sundays—I even made a goal out of writing letters once a month. I'd end up starting all these things with great enthusiasm and then drop them. It was as if none of them really meant anything to me.

"Then something quite wonderful happened. I was out jogging and I noticed a very old woman crossing a busy street at a snail's pace in a walker. I jogged straight over to her and assisted her on the rest of her belabored trek home. She was a delightful person and we exchanged phone numbers as we said good-bye. The rest of the day I was filled with a real sense of purpose—I had done something to make another person's life a little more pleasant and manageable.

"That very afternoon, I decided I wanted to work with older people in some way. I called several volunteer organizations and was directed to one that works with the elderly in my community. When I told them I was interested in being a volunteer, they told me they had a visiting neighbors program where volunteers helped elderly people without family live on their own and maintain independent life-styles. The position entailed providing companionship regularly, doing shopping and other errands, accompanying people to doctors' appointments, and other things of that nature. The next day I went to the volunteer office and signed up. It's six years later and I have been a loyal companion to several elderly people in my community ever since. I look forward to all of my visits and errands, and holidays mean more to me than they ever have since my family has grown manyfold.

"My volunteer work is by far the best goal I've ever made. The difference between it and the goals I haven't been able to reach is that my work with old people gives me a real sense of meaning in my life. I have a feeling of deep commitment to what I'm doing, which is what I call passion. The same three hours a week I used to dread when jogging, cycling, or cleaning my house are pure joy to me now because I love what I do."

Drive and Motivation

Out of the passion people feel for something comes the drive and motivation necessary for bringing it into their lives. With passion, motivation comes easily and naturally. Without passion, you have to work harder at getting motivated. The motivation you have for doing anything can be measured in direct proportion to how much you want it. Unlike passion, however, motivation is a little more manufacturable.

While speaking at an event in New Jersey, we met a single mother who worked as a bank teller and wanted to be promoted to a loan officer. She really didn't care whether she was a teller or a loan officer as far as the work involved, but she very much wanted the $100-a-week pay increase that came with the new position. When it came to making a plan about how to increase her chances of being singled out for promotion, she kept reminding herself how much she and her two children would benefit from the extra money.

With the extra motivation, she buckled down and followed the plan she came up with, which included perfect attendance and punctuality, staying after her shift every day to help with other tasks, going the extra measure to help and be personable to customers, and volunteering to train new employees. Within a year of setting her goal to be promoted, she reached it. The twist to the story is that instead of putting in for the loan officer position, she applied for teller supervisor—a position she really did like and that entitled her to an even greater pay raise!

In this case the woman lacked passion for her goal, but she found the motivation for pursuing and reaching it. The goal of getting promoted represented the larger goal of earning more money, which in turn represented the even larger goal of providing a more comfortable life for her and her children. Most goals share this quality of being greater than their face value.

The Road Map

Having a sense of direction about their lives is another trait most goal getters have in common. One woman we met put it this way: "When I get in my car, I have a destination in mind 95 percent of the time. Once in a while, I take a leisurely drive with no real place in mind, but the rest of the time I know exactly where I'm going. A few years ago I thought, 'Wouldn't it be great if I could be as sure about where I'm going in my life as I am when I'm driving?' From then on, I've tried to have that kind of sureness of direction and purpose in everything I do, which has given me a feeling of control over what happens to me, since I'm the one writing the agenda. So far, it's worked out about 95 percent of the time!"

Having a sense of direction about your life is important whether you are setting goals or not. Without direction, you make yourself too vulnerable to the whims of the various winds in life while driving around in circles. How often do we hear people bemoan the fact that they were victims of circumstance? "If only I could have gone to college," "If only I had waited to get married or have children," or "If only I had looked harder for a better job. . . ." We've all heard it or said it at some point in our lives. When you impose no sense of direction on your life, too often life steps in and directs it for you in whatever way it will.

As far as goals are concerned, a sense of direction is critical since most goals are tied into, and come out of, a larger life plan. Some goals have a specific, isolated purpose, as in the case of the woman who made a goal of volunteering her time to helping the elderly. A couple we met at a seminar in Arizona told a story about their extremely goal-oriented son, Mark.

Before Mark started junior high school, he had a goal: to get into a prestigious college preparatory high school. No sooner did he achieve that goal, he decided (at fourteen years old) he wanted to get into a premedical school program at Stanford University after high school. Having reached that goal, his new goal was to join the Peace Corps and practice medicine in a Third World country after finishing medical school, which is exactly what he is doing now. In between reaching all of his big goals, Mark had smaller, semester-by-semester goals of doing well academically and qualifying for scholarships so that all of his life dreams would one day come true. Astounded, people in the audience asked the couple what they did to encourage their son to be such a responsible and focused young person. They responded, "All we did was support and encourage the direction he had chosen for himself."

Discipline

Self-discipline is another pervasive trait among goal getters. Like Mark, goal getters are pretty good at putting a lot of effort into getting what they want. They are willing to work hard and sacrifice whatever pleasures may be had while applying themselves to reaching their goals. Young Doctor Mark most certainly must have given up many opportunities to be carefree during his formative years in order to devote himself to his studies. Part of why so many of us are goal setters instead of goal getters is that we are unwilling to put forth the time and toil needed to reach our goals.

It's ironic that in a society whose very beginnings are rooted in the work ethic, we have grown averse to working or, at least, averse to putting ourselves out any more than we have to. Unfortunately, we have all been lulled into that mind-set by mass advertisements that promise us a life of convenience from fast food to permanent-press clothing. But some do manage to buck the messages that bombard them and work very hard to make their dreams come true.

Commitment and Perseverance

Perhaps the most important ingredients of all that go into goal getting are commitment and perseverance. When we ask goal getters the secret to their success in reaching goals, nine out of ten say it's commitment. One especially memorable comment came from a real estate broker in her early sixties who likened goals to marriage. "If there's something you want, you have to get married to it, which means you have to be committed, devoted, and faithful. You have to show it respect by doing all the things necessary to make it happen. You can't be fickle and abandon it for whatever good-looking goal that comes along—unless all you want from life is a string of one-night stands. Marry your goal, trust it, be devoted to it, and put yourself on the line for it—that's what I do every time!"

It's interesting to note that our real estate broker friend was left by her husband when she was in her late twenties and raised their three children on her own. Having never worked or gone to college, she was at a total loss as to how to provide for herself and her children. She decided to make a life plan, which included several goals: getting a job, working her way through college, getting a job in real estate, becoming a broker, and owning her own real estate company. Not only did she achieve every one of her goals, she also sent each of her children to the college of their choice. In her spare time she goes sailing, paints, goes to flower shows (she's a proficient gardener), and volunteers her time to teach disadvantaged adults how to read—also goals she got married to along the way. By the way, the original name of her real estate company was "Fidelity."

The main reason we abandon our goals is a lack of commitment. How many of us are guilty of setting a goal, going at it gung ho, and then dropping it? Even something as ordinary as a New Year's resolution is hard to live up to. Whether we commit ourselves to our goals and persevere to attain them depends on whether or not we have the passion or motivation for going after them. It's obvious by now that goal getting entails a whole host of ingredients—just having them is not enough.

When you are setting a goal, take the time to sit down and imagine all the things that will go into reaching it and ask yourself if it is something you can realistically accomplish. When we aim for something that we are doomed to fail at for lack of desire, motivation, time, or any other reason, we create a negative experience about goals and take that feeling into the next goal we set. That's why it's so important to be selective about the goals you go after. Go after the ones that match who you really are and have something to do with what makes you tick. Be like a matchmaker and eliminate the ones that have nothing to do with who you are.

Flexibility

A rather interesting nuance we have noticed in personalities of goal getters is flexibility. For the most part they are open to new things and able to make the necessary changes in their lives for doing new things. We imagined that goal getters would be more rigid—those types that can stick to one thing and go at it with an unwavering focus. Yet the more people we talked with, the clearer it became that just the opposite is true. Rigid people tend to lock themselves into a habit of being, whereas flexible people are much more open to change. And in the final analysis, goals represent change—they are the vehicles we use to change our lives in some way.

A great example of flexibility is demonstrated in the story of John—a goal getter we met at a workshop in Denver who changed his whole life around to work himself up the ladder at a newspaper. Married, with one child, John had worked the day shift as a reporter for six years. He and his wife had fallen into a pretty comfortable pattern: dinner every night at 7:00 P.M., followed by playtime with their four-year-old daughter, a few hours of television, relaxing before bedtime, and sleep. On the weekend they would usually go on an excursion of some sort, visit relatives, or devote themselves to projects at home.

Then something happened. John was becoming a little restless at work. Besides getting a bit burned out from the daily drain of reporting people's tragedies, he began sensing a need to move on, to grow. One day it was announced that the news editor was retiring and the current assistant news editor would be filling that spot, which meant the assistant news editor position was open. John immediately saw the opening as his chance to move up and on. The problem, however, was that the new desk hours were from 5:00 P.M. to 1:00 A.M., and the assistant news editor had to work weekends to fill in for the news editor, who had weekends off.

John discussed his dilemma with his wife, since her life would be very much affected if he was selected for the position. After a lot of kicking and screaming, she gave in, realizing that John wouldn't be very much fun if he carried around a feeling of dissatisfaction. He applied for the spot and was chosen. His day-to-day routine was thrown on its head: he left for work at 4:30 P.M., got home around 2:00 A.M., fell asleep at 4:00 A.M., woke up at noon, did chores and helped care for their daughter before work, and he and his wife and daughter took trips and made visits on Mondays and Tuesdays (his new days off). He also performed an entirely different function at work.

For John to make the change successfully, he had to be flexible about practically everything in his life. The payoff? John felt as if he was growing, he made advancement possible, and no longer felt as if he was pigeonholed into one job or one way of life. He was flexible enough to make his goal a reality. Today, we might add, John is the news editor at his paper and has his sights on the assistant managing editor spot. And although he still works the night shift, he has weekends off.

Tunnel Vision

Goal getters also have a gift for putting on blinders when going after their goals. They zero in on something and go for it. Years ago a friend of ours had his heart set on becoming a special agent in the FBI. He was a certified public accountant and although he made good money, he found his work a bit dull. He had always dreamed about having an adventurous career, but never really knew what. He stumbled across an ad in the newspaper that said the FBI was recruiting accountants, lawyers, and scientists. A bell went off and he wrote the recruiting office and asked for an application. After passing an initial screening, he was asked to come in and take a battery of tests, which he did. Having passed them, the next step was to get himself into physical shape so that he could pass a rather rigorous physical fitness exam, which he would be required to take in three to six months.

He learned that the test required him to run two miles in about seventeen minutes, as well as run an obstacle course, sit-ups, push-ups, pull-ups, and a body flexibility test—all in a fixed amount of time. He also had to meet a weight and body fat standard. Having been rather sedentary in his desk job at an accounting firm, his work was cut out for him. He joined a gym and worked out every day. His workouts included all the things that would be on the test, as well as weight lifting, rowing, cycling, and swimming. In three months he had converted fifteen pounds of fat into muscle and had the endurance of a cross-country skier. Five months after he began his workouts, he was called to take a fitness test at Roosevelt Island in New York.

As fit as he was, he was unable to finish the two-mile run in the minimum time, which caused him to fail the test. He did well enough on the rest of the tests to qualify for being recalled to take the test again, but he wasn't told when it would be. From that day on, he stayed with his same daily exercise regime, but increased his run to five miles a day. He set one day a week aside to run two miles as fast as he could. Within a month and a half, he could complete the run in a little more than sixteen minutes—which put him in the fastest category by FBI standards. He wasn't notified to take another fitness test for six more months, but when he was, he passed with flying colors. In three more months, he was called down to the FBI Academy in Quantico, Virginia, where he would go through intense academic and physical training for sixteen weeks.

Our friend wanted something and he kept his sights on his goal for nearly two years! He has been with the FBI as a special agent for ten years now, and finds much adventure and job satisfaction while uncovering white collar crimes in corporations and conducting undercover investigations of money-laundering schemes.

Realistic Expectations

Often, when we set goals, we aim at the stars, which most of the time ends up to be our undoing. Most all of the goal getters that we've met reach for something that is within their grasp. The woman who wanted to work with the elderly didn't try to become a social worker, she volunteered her time while leaving the rest of her life intact. Too, she didn't overextend herself by volunteering ten hours a week, she limited it to three. In short, she increased the likelihood of reaching her goal by keeping it reachable.

Likewise, the woman who wanted to be promoted at her

bank didn't apply for the promotion until she had set the more immediate goals of increasing her day-to-day performance in the position she had. By making herself stand out as a model employee, she set the stage for getting singled out for promotion. The young man who wanted to be a doctor focused on attaining his goal step by step—by doing what he needed to do in the present to pave the way to making his loftiest goal possible. All of these goal getters have been able to limit their sights to what was possible—they didn't overwhelm themselves from the start, as is so often the case.

Having realistic expectations is an integral part of getting what we want. Also, setting goals can be intimidating, which is all the more reason to start slow and go about reaching your goals in steps. Once you've figured out what you want, think of all the little steps—reachable goals—you can take to get it. Besides not overwhelming yourself, this strategy helps ignite a momentum. Accomplishing little goals propels you to the next goal, which, in turn, sets the stage for success at achieving the next and the next. Before you know it, the larger goals are within your grasp.

This and That About Goals

Having looked at the traits that most of the goal getters we've known have in common, we'd like to spend a little time on some miscellaneous thoughts about goals. The first thing we'd like to stress is that having goals is paramount to having control of your life. If you don't take control of your life, someone or something else will. It's your life, you should be the one writing the agenda. Goals, in short, are the "to do" list for your life!

The next thing, which gets at the very core of what this book is all about, is that goals are a valuable means to achieve personal and professional satisfaction. Up to now we have focused on a primarily inward journey. The more you know about yourself, the better you will be at setting goals. Hopefully, with your increased self-knowledge, you will be able to zero in on goals that are right for you. Many ask, "How do you go about setting the right goals?" "What is the key to knowing what they are?" *You* are the key, and finding out what makes you tick is the door to unlock! You have to know who you are to know what you want. Too many of us chase after someone else's goals, a pursuit that is doomed to failure from the start. Setting goals is the most important step in making your dreams to be who you most want to be come true. Remember, each goal you meet lays the foundation for future growth and success, and an ever-increasing sense of personal fulfillment.

Once you've landed on goals that are important to you, it is necessary to sit down and map out a strategy for reaching them. First look at what motivation exists for each particular goal. The stronger your motivation, the easier it will be to come up with a strategy. Where your motivation is weak, manufacture extra motivation by looking at all the ways reaching your goal will affect your life. For example, if you want to go back to college and get your degree because it's something you've always wanted, but your motivation is weak because you already have a good job that you enjoy, then look at other ways in which finishing your education will benefit your life. Not only will it give you personal satisfaction, it will also make you more knowledgeable, broaden your interests and curiosity, make you more interesting, as well as open up doors to other jobs or promotions down the road.

The most important thing in planning your strategy is to keep your goals manageable. Be realistic in your expectations, as we've already talked about. Guard against overextending yourself from the outset. Create a realistic timetable, as well. If you are working full-time and want to go back to school, don't schedule classes every night of the week. Start out with one or two a week and get a couple of semesters behind you. Too often people become frustrated, thinking that their goal will take forever, so they overwhelm themselves by attempting to accomplish it within an unrealistic time frame. It's better that your goals take forever and are reached than to approach them with too much haste and fail.

A comment we hear frequently is, "I set goals but something always gets in the way!" The more we probed, it became clear that the people saying this always seem to get in their own way. If you don't put blinders on, something will always get in the way. It's up to you to put them on and keep them on! If you don't, you will always be your biggest obstacle. You have to look at the walls you've put up before you can tear them down.

Another comment we hear a lot is, "I'm just not a goal-oriented person." The people who say this are those whom we call "quick quitters." Some people simply don't want to put forth the effort to go about getting their goals and, in the end, they just don't want them enough. Instead of calling it like it is, they rationalize giving up on their goals by saying that they aren't goal-oriented. We want to stress that not going after goals does not make you any less of a person—it doesn't. It does, however, make you vulnerable to other forces controlling your life, as well as cutting short your chances for personal fulfillment.

One last thing about goals is that often people do not think they are amenable to change. The truth is, they are! There is nothing wrong with changing your mind *or* your goals. As a matter of fact, it's better to abandon a goal you've realized is not right for you and spend your time on a new goal that is. Sometimes what we really need to do is simply change our goals around a little. A friend of ours started out in college studying drama with the hope of one day writing plays. Her love of drama grew and grew, but she realized midstream that she was much more interested in directing plays than writing them. Instead of abandoning her goal of being a dramatist, she realigned it and concentrated her energy on directing. Adding new information to your goal can be very constructive, and is by no means a basis to give it up!

Goalposts

Over the years we have asked our audiences to describe in one word what objectives they've wanted their goals to satisfy. We will share the list with you and ask you to come up with your own word to add to the list.

- Adventure
- Freedom
- Growth
- Risk
- Money
- Challenge
- Fulfillment
- Security
- Recognition
- Respect
- Health
- Family
- Values
- Relaxation
- Knowledge
- Romance
- Power
- Balance

- Ego
- Friends
- Your word(s)?

Notes to Yourself

Goals often start out as dreams and end up as broken promises. But with awareness, commitment, persistence, and a strategy, goals can be the means by which dreams come true. Here are some questions to start you on your way. Please write down your answers.

- What goals have you set for yourself in the past?
- Which ones have you reached?
- Which ones haven't you reached?
- What do these past goals tell you about yourself?
- What goal would you make for yourself today?
- Why did you choose this particular goal?
- What does your goal say about who you are?
- What would help you achieve your goal?
- What would stop you from achieving your goal?
- What is the first step you can take toward your goal?
- What is the second step?

Take a few minutes to reflect on what you've just done. Write your goal down on a piece of paper and keep it with you. Put a copy of it on your bathroom mirror, on your refrigerator, and in your wallet. Jot down realistic strategies for reaching it. Remember, realistic goal setters can be successful goal getters.

PART II

YOU AGAINST THE WORLD

Risk! Risk anything! Care no more for the opinions of others. . . . Do the hardest thing on earth for you. Act for yourself.

—*Katherine Mansfield*

It has been said that the greatest measure of our lives is our actions. And the best fruit of our knowledge is how that knowledge affects movement in our lives. At this point we hope you have thought a good deal about yourself and your life—what makes you tick, what it means to believe in yourself, how to define success, and what goes into setting goals that are right for you. You are in the driver's seat. It is time to avert your glance from the rearview window and look at what lies ahead. It's time to plot your direction and get going—time to act.

As you chart the course for the rest of your life, take heed of what we consider to be the Ten Most Important Two-Letter Words: "If It Is To Be, It Is Up To Me!" We dare you now to get out of your established comfort zone, and stretch yourself like a rubber band and see how broad and elastic you really are! Take your dreams out of the spinning wheel and, with them, pave the road in front of you. Find a strategy for keeping each goal along the way reachable, and don't try to cover too much ground at once. Your journey is ongoing—don't rush through it. Take in the landscape, the color of the horizon, and the shape of the clouds.

Most important, get started! Remember the words of Robert Frost, "There are those who talk of going but never get away. Someday I'll have less to say but I'll be gone."

Chapter Five

Charting Your Course

Act, act in the living present, heart within, and God overhead.

—*Henry Wadsworth Longfellow*

In the last chapter we talked about all the things that go into getting goals. Now we'd like not only to help you find strategies to get your goals, but also to help you put them in the framework of a life plan. As you begin charting your course and reaching the goals that go into fulfilling your life plan, remember that it's a solo journey. We are here to help you, like coaches, but nobody but you can put forth the daily effort needed to turn your goals into real accomplishments. In the same way, nobody but you can make your life what you most want it to be. Nobody but you can take the steps to the top of the stairway of your dreams. Nobody but you will give you a nudge on the shoulder and say, "Get going!"

The All-Importance of Strategy

We talked indirectly about goal-getting strategies in the last chapter. Now we think it will be most helpful to talk about them specifically. We have chosen to focus on various successful strategies different people we've met have used to attain their goals. Our selection of stories reflects a range of people and jobs. Try to identify with scenarios that best reflect you and your life, and borrow strategies that you think might work for you.

Mapmaking

Remember the woman we spoke of in the last chapter, who decided to treat her life like driving? She thought if she could be as directed in her life as she was while she was driving, she'd have a destination in mind 95 percent of the time. Having stumbled upon that realization, she developed a "mapping" strategy to just about everything she does. Not only does she map out all her daily plans, she maps out weekly, monthly, and yearly plans as well. She literally draws maps! A typical daily map consists of "Point A" (the starting point) with arrows jutting out to various other points that represent the goals she has set for the day.

A goal for the day might be a specific task or errand, meeting a friend for lunch or dinner, helping her children with their homework, reading, exercising, or some other discrete activity. Weekly goals might consist of finishing a book, exercising five hours, earning five hours of overtime at work, or finishing a particular project at home. Yearly goals might include saving a certain sum of money, learning something new—such as Greek history or golf—traveling, and entertaining friends once a month. The maps take on whatever shape is needed to satisfy her planned accomplishments. Often her maps include notes to herself in the form of road signs! She also posts speed limits to guard against running out of gas!

Her life plan map is an intricate creation in process. Its sprawling branches of veins resemble the face of a very old Navajo. Designed after the United States, each state represents a year in her life. Her life goals include retiring from teaching when she is fifty-five, buying an ocean-front home on the West Coast and relocating there, assisting her three children through college, and writing articles for educational journals. She knows exactly what she wants to do with her life, which, she says, gives her a very comforting feeling of control.

One attendee at the seminar where she showed her maps asked if there was any room for spontaneity in her life. She quickly pointed to her life map: "See these red lines? Those are the back roads I can travel if the highways become too monotonous." She had even penciled in a route for detours! Though her example can easily be considered extreme, if not compulsive, we found our friend's map strategy to goal getting totally ingenious, individualistic, and, most important, effective.

Rewards and Punishments

Most of the successful goal strategists we've met have not been quite as creative as the mapmaker, but one very memorable goal getter devised a comprehensive strategy for her life plan through an elaborate system of rewards and punishments. Her rule is very simple: "If I do what I set out to do, I reward myself; if I don't, I pay a penalty." After asking this thirty-two-year-old office manager for examples of how her system worked, she described it in detail:

"It started when I failed at another diet. I was always overweight and always on one diet or another—I've tried them all. I would always feel pretty miserable when I would go off a diet—as if I were a failure. And I hated feeling like I had to start all over again. I felt like I was climbing the same mountain over and over and would never make it to the top. The whole thing seemed like a terrible punishment. Then it occurred to me that since I was already feeling as if I were being punished, why didn't I really punish myself? Besides, nothing could be as bad as feeling like a constant failure!

"That's when I came up with a plan. I decided that every time I went off my diet, I would take something away from myself—like going out with my friends on the weekend, something I really love to do. And if I met my goal of losing twenty pounds, I'd reward myself with something real special and out of the ordinary—like going to California for a long weekend. The first time I went off my diet I stuck to my guns and canceled all my weekend plans. It was unbearable! I've just never been the kind of person who enjoys being alone. In fact, sometimes I feel as if I live for the time I have with the people I love.

"The next week staying on my diet was easy—anything was more tolerable than spending another weekend alone doing nothing! I stayed on my diet for the next nine weeks, which was when I lost the twenty pounds. That was a first for me. The longest I had lasted on a diet was about four weeks, and I never lost more than ten pounds. I booked a trip to California with two of my best friends and had the time of my life!

"I used the same strategy to maintain my weight. If I gained more than two pounds, it meant solitary confinement. Feeling a lot more self-confident, since I was no longer thinking of myself as a failure, I started applying my strategy to other goals. One of my goals was to read more books, so every time I finished one, I'd put $10 in my savings account toward a trip to Mexico. If I took more than two weeks to finish a book, I'd take $10 out of my savings. Before I knew it, I was reading in all my spare time. Ironically, reading turned out to be a great way for me to learn how to enjoy spending more time by myself. I had to change the way I maintained my diet since spending a weekend alone wasn't such a horrible thing anymore. If I gained two pounds I forced myself to exercise an hour a day, something I truly dreaded!

"My next goal was to get promoted from my position as receptionist to office manager. I practiced typing every night at home until I was up to seventy words per minute, and I also took a writing class at night school to improve my communication skills. I even gave myself spelling and grammar drills at home. If I slacked off at all, I wouldn't make plans for the weekend and wouldn't allow myself any pleasure reading! I got the promotion within six months. All my new goals got me to think more seriously about my life than I ever had before. Everything seemed to be opening up, possibilities were abundant. I forced myself to the inevitable question: 'What do I want from the rest of my life?' The answer, surprisingly, came pretty easily—I wanted to go to college and become a nurse.

"Now I am almost halfway through my nursing program, have been to Mexico, and am no longer an ounce overweight. When I get my degree and get a job in the health profession, I plan to settle down and get married and have kids—something I've wanted as long as I can remember and something I fully expect to have."

Strategic Advice

Strategy is by far the most important ingredient that goes into taking a goal from the planning stage to the action stage. It is the very footwork of turning goals into accomplishments. Sometimes it's hard to remove ourselves from our day-to-day routines long enough to envision a life plan and possible strategies by which to go after it. Many people we have met have found it helpful to seclude themselves for a few hours with their thoughts, a pen, and paper. We met a woman at a seminar in Hartford, Connecticut, who worked in insurance sales. She was recently divorced and decided that she wanted to relocate to Phoenix, where a few friends of hers lived. Being too easily distracted at home, she took herself out to dinner and spent several hours jotting down the steps that would take her and her children to Phoenix.

A couple we know told us that when they were driving from New York to Boston, they ended up drafting a blueprint for their future. The wife said, "Okay, it's time to get real! We're going to do what we've been promising to do for the last ten years—talk about our life!" Her husband asked, "Now?" She retorted, "We'll be prisoners in the car for the next eight hours, I can't think of a better time." That was the moment their journey really began.

We cannot stress enough the importance of taking these kinds of critical time-outs. It is equally important to cheer yourself on with positive, constructive, can-do thoughts. Negative thinking is a terrible roadblock to action. How many times do people talk themselves out of something before they even begin? Too many! You need to believe that what you want is possible. If you don't, your dreams will wind up in the valley of unrealized hopes, where they become paper-thin and disappear. If you don't believe in your dreams, don't even bother with your plan—it will never come true if you are not 100 percent behind it. William Carlos Williams wrote in one of his poems, "Reality is born in the imagination," which is a truism we live by and urge you to also. Imagining what's possible is what makes something possible—it's like creating a first draft in your mind's eye.

Imagine

Another effective technique some people use to take their goals from the plan stage to the action stage is to mentally walk through them. Imagine yourself in every stage of your plan. Highlight the details. If your plan means relocating to another area, imagine yourself taking the real steps involved: putting your home up for sale, giving notice at your job, trying out your new location on a test basis, leaving your present area, living without certain friends or family in your life on a regular basis, imagining the climate of your new location from season to season, imagining a new job and new people in your life, and what kind of day-to-day life your new location will offer.

Likewise, if your plan involves making a job or career change, imagine all the details of your new work role—your responsibilities, new coworkers, environment, what you enjoy about it, the challenges, how you will dress, what you don't enjoy about it, and where you can go from there. By walking through your plan mentally, it takes on a "real" shape. It also helps take some of the anxiety out of the plan because the picture you've formed makes the changes seem familiar and less foreign.

A plan for your life is like a blueprint to a house or a map to a given destination. As we were writing this chapter, heavy-weight boxer Riddick Bowe beat World Heavyweight Champion Evander Holyfield. One of the headlines in a New York newspaper read, "Living His Dream." In the article members of Riddick's family were quoted as saying, "He had it in him from the start, he was the one with the plan." When asked about what his family had said, Riddick responded, "I just take my dreams one by one."

As you go forward in your plan of action, we ask you to be your own cheerleader and join your own PEP squad. Approach your life plan with plenty of PEP—perseverance, enthusiasm, and patience—to keep yourself going when the going gets rough. Getting what you want in life isn't easy. It means sticking to a game plan and never losing sight of your immediate and future happiness. Staying focused will be challenging, to say the least, because there will be many distractions to meet you along the way. There's a saying in real estate that the three most important things are "location, location, location." Likewise, the three most important things in fulfilling a life plan are "focus, focus, focus!"

When distractions do come along and tempt you off your path, put blinders on—racehorses are fitted with blinders to ensure that they see nothing but the track in front of them. Remind yourself you're in this race to win! Blinders can block out the obvious distractions of time, other opportunities, and momentary pleasures, but one woman we met said she wore blinders to block out her sister! Her sister, she said, always belittled her. She criticized her ambitions, her way of life, and even the way she dressed. Instead of giving in to her sister's attempts to undermine her life and direction, she ignored her. Luckily, too, she believed in herself enough not to be undermined! It's very important to learn how to tune out negative voices.

Another woman we met at one of our seminars said she had trouble putting her needs in front of everyone else's. All her life she catered to others, and it felt like a habit much too ingrained to shake off. After a long goal-writing session, she was the first one to complete her list of goals! She remarked, "It's as if they were just waiting to burst out. After so many years of pushing them down, they came up like a volcanic eruption!" When it came to creating a plan, however, she just sat in her chair and twirled her pencil absentmindedly—she was stumped. Unfortunately, she wasn't alone—most of us do feel stumped when it comes to finding a plan to turn our goals into real actions.

When it comes to drafting your plan, try to keep it simple to start. Recite the "CBA's of life—conceive, believe, and achieve—and stay keyed into those three magic words. Aim at goals that are within your reach, and choose goals that can be aligned to take you ever nearer to fulfilling your life plan. It's an exciting feeling to know that you are working to create your own future. Not only do you get a feeling of deep satisfaction and anticipation from knowing you are going after the life you want, but also a feeling of relief in knowing that your life is not snowballing into something you don't want. Be ever vigilant to fine-tune your goals so that they are graspable and that they help pave the way to the future you want.

Minor Adjustments

We met Joe at a two-day seminar in Southern California three years ago. Joe described himself as "the world's worst goalie." He made this comment about himself while expressing how futile his past efforts had been in reaching his goals. "I set them, then I break them. It's as if there's a circuit missing in my brain!" After a little probing we found out that Joe, a sales manager at a major retail clothing store chain, earns $30,000 a year. After asking for an example of a failed goal, he said, "Saving $10,000 a year."

We suggested to Joe that he modify his expectations and aim at a goal that is more reachable, such as saving $2,000 a year or, better yet, $40 a week. Not only is $2,000 a year more realistic, it is more affordable—$10,000 is one-third of Joe's income, whereas $2,000 is one-fifteenth! And by aiming at $40 a week, the goal becomes more immediate and real. Being in closer proximity to a goal makes one's commitment to it stronger, which increases the chances of reaching it.

Our next question to Joe was why saving money was an important goal to him. He answered that he had always wanted to build his own log cabin in the mountains. Our remark to him was that his goal fit into a larger life plan. A look of surprise lit up his face and he said, "It never occurred to me to look at it that way, but that's exactly it. It's funny, I never thought I had a life plan—I always thought of building a cabin as just something I wanted to do."

With a little goal modification and clarification, Joe's impossible goal of saving a huge sum of money each year turned into a much more manageable goal of a saving a modest sum of money each week. With the framework of a life plan, Joe has since set more goals to help him get closer to that log cabin in the mountains. He has taken some home-building courses, has read books and articles on building cabins, has taken trips to search for the ideal location, and has applied for jobs in different mountainous regions.

Test Marketing Your Plan

A social worker friend of ours thought of leaving social services to go to law school. He investigated law schools and what financial assistance was available. After submitting applications to various schools, he planned to resign from his job so he could go to school full-time. We asked him why he was interested in law and he admitted that he was mainly interested in making more money. We voiced concern that the goal might not be strong enough to warrant taking such drastic measures. We asked if he had thought of testing the waters first—taking a class at night to see if he liked it before turning his life upside down. He heeded our advice and signed up for one night class. Not only did he hate the class, he was totally turned off to the profession. For the time being, our friend has decided to stay in social work while taking a close look at what he really wants.

Making it Happen

Another friend of ours was promoted recently to an executive position at a light manufacturing company. Upon congratulating him, he said, "I'd rather you be congratulating me on owning my own nursery!" Bewildered by his comment, we looked at each other and then back at him. He went on to tell us that his life dream has been to run his own nursery and tree farm. He confessed that the older he got, the more he thought about it. He even hinted that he was beginning to regret his life for not having pursued his dream when he was younger.

Sensing the urgency of what he was going through, we invited him to dinner and he spent the whole evening laying his dream out on the table. We got him to review his financial picture to see what he could afford. We suggested that he start looking in the Sunday want ads, talk to people who were in the business, and look into getting a small business loan. He was so psyched that he and his wife stayed up all night talking about what it would take to hitch onto his star. She said, "I wondered when you'd be ready!"

Over the weeks that followed, he spoke to numerous people in the business. During a conversation with the owner of the nursery where he had bought his gardening supplies for the last fifteen years, the owner revealed that he was thinking of retiring soon and moving to Florida. Bingo! He lined up a loan, gave notice at his manufacturing plant, remortgaged his and his wife's house, hired his wife on a part-time basis, and bought the nursery. Today, he is the owner of Chelsea Farms. More importantly, he is the owner of his dreams!

Manuscript Test

Take a moment to look at your life as a book—a manuscript in progress—and imagine yourself as a critic reviewing it. Ask a critic's questions: "Is it good? Does it work? What are its strong points? How is it weak? Did it do what it set out to do? Does it get a thumbs-up?" Now imagine that you are the editor of that very same book. What pointers would you give to the writer to make it better? What parts would you suggest be eliminated, what parts added? What direction would you aim it in to make it earn a thumbs-up? Where does your book go from here? Nobody but you can be the critic of the book of your life. Nobody but you can answer the question "Is it all that I want it to be?"

Final Thoughts

When charting your course, ask yourself, "What do I want to be doing a year from now? Five years? Ten years? Twenty years?" It really is in your power to decide what mile posts you want to reach. You don't have to passively await what the years will hand down to you. By setting goals and putting them into a framework of a life plan, you become the boss of time, while it waits on you like a humble servant. It's awesome to know that the power over our lives is in our hands—we really can decide what happens to us! It's such a simple realization, yet it's baffling to think that it so often floats right over our heads! How many of us are truly living the lives that we most want to live? How many not-so-satisfying things do we let fill our days, our years? Some of them are unavoidable, but certainly not all. How often are we truly filled with a happy and excited feeling about being alive?

Let this last spark of awareness be your catalyst for seizing the day! Take stock of your life and put it back into your own hands!

Set your goals, whatever they may be—job change or advancement, relocating, marriage, divorce, having a child, saving money, going to school, learning something new, or buying a home. Work to turn them into accomplishments that will bring you joy, satisfaction, and open the door to tomorrow. Plant your life plan with the seeds of today's goals and watch it sprout up from the ground like a beautiful, life-bearing flower. Nurture it, groom it, and let its beauty bring you pleasure in all your years to come.

Chapter Six

Focusing on Resources

Every chapter so far has had one thing in common—you! Finding resources to help you get what you want depends on you, too. There are many avenues available to assist you in getting what you want, but it is up to you to seek them out and put them to use. Besides effort, you also have to knock on the door of your imagination before you can enter the realm of available opportunities. There is no ready-made list of resources available to help you along your journey—you have to tailor-make your own. What we offer you here is a starting point, ideas that can head you in a particular direction. From there, it is up to you to maximize what you find. What follows are the Six P's—people, public, paper, practical, particular, and personal resources.

People Resources

Three addresses will always inspire confidence . . .
—*Oscar Wilde*

The resource people use most often is other people. Whether your aim is a job promotion, job change, relocation, college entry or reentry, or whatever else, contacting the right people is vital. Not only is it important access to finding out who knows whom, but sometimes just talking to people who are doing, or have done, what it is you want to do is extremely helpful. Besides serving as role models, people wearing the hat you want to wear can offer critical insight on how they did it, how they do it, and their satisfaction level. Making contacts— getting on the inside track of the who knows whom—is probably the most immediate resource that will get you connected to what you want.

Whom, exactly, are we talking about? What people? If you are aiming at a vertical move at work, say, from executive secretary to assistant to the vice president of a corporation, talk to other assistants to VPs. Ask them how they got where they are, what jobs they came from, what experience or background was required of them to secure their position, special training or skills, whom they talked to, what channels they used, and whom they knew. Ask specific questions, such as what interview questions were asked, how they found out about the opening, what the position entails, and what they like and dislike about it.

Perhaps the information you receive will lead you in a particular direction. For example, you may find out that all the assistants to VPs you spoke with have something in common, such as a background in communications. And if you don't have such a background, maybe the next logical step for you to take is to make a lateral transfer to a secretarial spot in the communications department to increase your chances of securing an assistant-to-the-VP position down the road. We have found this kind of information-getting to be very useful.

Role models are frequently used people resources. Often people attribute their success at a particular pursuit or vocation to a certain role model in their lives. Having seen someone achieve something is great inspiration for achieving it yourself.

Even reading biographies can offer vicarious role models. We met a woman in Louisville, Kentucky, who started her own printing business. Before she did, she worked part-time for two years at the best print shop in Louisville and learned everything she could directly from the owner. "As well as learning what to do, I learned what not to do. I saved a lot of money doing it this way, because my own mistakes would have been costly!"

Forming Ongoing Alliances

It is also important to maintain and tap into the various alliances you've made throughout your life. It's surprising how many times just knowing the right people helps you get what you want, especially jobwise. If you haven't made it a practice to stay in contact with past coworkers, schoolmates, teachers, friends, family, people in organizations you may have belonged to or come into contact with at some time, start now. Keep a Rolodex or address book solely for that purpose. When the need arises, don't be shy about calling someone for help. Be prepared to ask for help and be specific about what you want. If someone can't help you directly, maybe he or she can lead you in the direction of someone who can. If you've lost touch with old friends and affiliates, renew contact by sending a card during the holidays.

While giving a luncheon talk on networking recently, someone told a great "I-knew-someone-who-knew-someone-else" story. When John was working his way through college, he decided that instead of working at McDonald's, busing tables, or tutoring, he would love to work on a salmon boat out of the Berkeley or San Francisco marinas. He didn't have a clue as to how to go about finding such a job, so he decided to call a distant cousin in Maine who he had remembered his family saying was a commercial fisherman.

Having made contact, his cousin said to go to the tackle and bait store at the San Francisco marina because his company frequently ordered tackle supplies there. Taking that lead, John went to the tackle and bait store and told the owner that So-and-So had sent him to ask about getting a job as a hand on a fishing boat for the summer. Sure enough, the owner knew of a salmon boat skipper who was looking for a deckhand! John left his phone number and the salmon boat skipper called in a few days. John got the job.

Public Resources

Related to people resources are public resources. These may include alumni associations, schools and colleges, trade and professional organizations, job fairs, job placement centers on college campuses, libraries, government offices, not-for-profit organizations, political action centers, churches and syna-gogues, public radio and television broadcast stations, human resources departments, state chambers of commerce, mu-seums, and on and on.

Often simply calling any one of these places can either pro-vide the information you want or lead you in the right direc-tion. Some libraries, post offices, and government offices, for example, post jobs and dates for civil service exams. Each subject department at colleges and universities posts jobs in related fields, and college career placement centers offer an abundance of job listings. Many placement centers do profiles to match your qualifications with available jobs or jobs ideal for your background.

If you're planning to relocate and want more information about a particular place or a list of possible ideal places, write or visit a state's chamber of commerce. These lists often rate cities and towns for habitability in terms of climate, roads and public transportation, city services, employment, geographical hazards such as earthquakes, tornadoes, floods, and hurricanes, and other conditions.

Paper Resources

Another valuable resource is published material. There are reams and reams of information on paper in the form of books, articles, indexes, catalogs, newsletters and other organization publications, reports, fact sheets, patents, records, tests, and on ad infinitum. Most libraries are good places to start, but some information can only be obtained by contacting a specific organization. Remember the retail sales manager who wanted to build a log cabin? His primary resource was books on how to do it! In fact, how do most people learn anything? Books! What is a college education? Mostly a lot of reading!

We heard of an independent corporate communications specialist who would network among friends specifically to obtain newsletters from major corporations. She would ask So-and-So who worked at Such-and-Such corporation to send her the company newsletter. She would also ask her friend to contact one of her friends at another company and ask for that company's newsletters. In time, she had acquired an extensive library of corporate newsletters.

From her newsletter library, she made a list of who's who at each company, became familiar with the company's projects and plans (as well as the industry jargon), did the necessary research to gain knowledge about each industry and specific projects, and eventually wrote letters to relevant higher-ups offering her services. Needless to say, she built quite a clientele for herself, and has since slowed down on gathering newsletters since she has all the work she can handle!

Practical Resources

By practical resources we mean those that have to do with experience. Internships, volunteer work in a particular field, schooling, summer jobs, hobbies—any type of hands-on experience with what it is you are thinking about doing. Jean-Jacques Rousseau wrote that formal education is unnecessary—that the best education derives from experience. If you are thinking of changing jobs or professions, try to test out your desired hat by trying it on in some way.

Remember our friend who almost left social work to go to law school? He decided to test the waters first by taking one night class and was totally turned off. More often than not, however, test marketing gives us affirmation for our choices. A woman who attended a talk we gave told how in her desire to get off the fast track she gradually introduced change into her life. As a successful, well-to-do New York stock market broker, she craved to have more in her life than money and investments.

Having no idea what would add more meaning to her life, she tried a little of a lot of things, such as traveling, writing, kayaking, and teaching inner-city children how to read on Saturdays. She instantly fell in love with teaching, and started taking courses in education at night. Within three years she completed her master's, applied for certification, and began contacting schools for a full-time position.

Schools are a tremendous practical resource, whether taking a class or enrolling in a course of study for a vocation or avocation. Classical Greek thinking about education was to view it as the ideal way to spend one's leisure time. How many of us have taken classes for the joy of learning something? Not nearly enough! Most modern cultures view education as a means to an end—specifically, a job. But it is also an invaluable means by which we can become broader, more fulfilled individuals.

Avocations, too, often turn into vocations. We heard an interesting story about a woman who took up coin collecting. Her interest was sparked after a friend had given her some old coins as a birthday gift. She bought a coin book to look up the value of the coins and found it so interesting that she read it from cover to cover. Next came coin magazines, more books, more coins, currency, encyclopedias, auction catalogs from rare coin shops—there was no stopping her. She went to coin shows, auctions, coin shops, and flea markets searching for rare finds.

She bought loupes and lamps and would peer at her coins for hours looking for minting errors, discerning condition, classifying. She was a numismatic natural! A free-lance writer by profession, she started writing about her discoveries and classifications and sent her articles to various coin publications. Her articles were not only accepted, they were applauded. Within a year she was writing about coins full-time! She also started a small mail-order coin business on the side.

Particular Resources

There are also many channels of assistance available to help people with specific situations, which are what we call particular resources. Getting help to get out of debt, for example, is relying on a particular resource. In the wake of the loose spending in the '80s, getting out of debt is a particular concern in the '90s—especially for those who have lost their jobs. Getting out of debt doesn't necessarily mean you have to file for bankruptcy and destroy your credit rating. There are government-sponsored consumer credit protection agencies in each state designed specifically to help consumers manage their debt without damaging their credit standing.

There are also many school loan forgiveness programs available to cancel or reduce the amount of school loan debt by filling a critical job niche. Health care professionals can have their loans forgiven by making a commitment to working in economically depressed areas where few doctors go voluntarily; new teachers are eligible for loan forgiveness by working in bilingual, inner-city schools; and even many police departments offer loan forgiveness as a way to attract educated people into law enforcement careers. With a little research, particular resources are often just a few phone calls away.

A young man we met at a seminar in Houston told the group how he came from a family of frustrated inventors, and how he was able to break out of the mold. Not that he wasn't an inventor, too, he just wasn't a frustrated one! He managed a car dealership for a living, and in his daydreams was always thinking up clever contraptions for various things. He kept an ongoing "idea" file, and one day called the U.S. Office of Patents in Washington, D.C., to see if it would send him some information about how to go about patenting an idea. The office referred him to a private organization called the Idea Center, also in Washington, which sent him a step-by-step workbook on how to patent and market his inventions. Since then he has three patents for items ranging from automobile accessories to beauty products packaging!

Therapists, rabbis, priests, and ministers can be tremendous particular people resources in a special time of need.

Personal Resources

Personal resources are all the things you yourself bring to the task of getting what you want. The imagination, intelligence, common sense, effort, past experience, knowledge, and attitude that you use to pursue your plans have a great bearing on whether or not you fulfill them. Unless you imagine the resources that are available to you, and spend time and effort to seek them out, you won't get past the ground floor.

Past accomplishments and successes are valuable resources in that they are a source of confidence you can draw on to reach your ever-evolving new goals and plans. What strengths did you draw on in past successful endeavors? Draw on those same strengths now while aiming at something else! Even past failures can be good teachers by offering insight into what to avoid or do differently in the future. It's up to you—how creative you can be with your own abilities and personal history.

We've noticed how so many of the people we've met in our groups have a problem looking beyond their own little worlds. They tend to see the world through a microscope and are unable, through habit, to unleash their imaginations long enough to see the multitudinous resources around them. In this case we often suggest that they take off their blinders and look at the world as if they were looking through a wide-angle lens!

A common reaction our clients have to these kinds of challenges we put to them is "Yeah, but, what if. . . ." That expression of hesitation is so popular, in fact, that we decided to confront it with yet another challenge—the "What If Test." In the test we ask people to replace a "what if" negative with a "what if" positive. For example, "What if I fail?" gets turned into "What if I succeed?" or "What if I lose all my money?" becomes "What if I double or triple my money!" Changing the negative "what if" mind-set is difficult, but it's amazing how an awareness of that mind-set makes it so less automatic. At the very least the "What If Test" opens eyes to a new way of viewing what's possible.

Positive thinking, which we think is part of attitude, is a very important personal resource. So often when we think something is possible, we make it possible—the very expectation of something paves the way to its reality. How many times have we gotten what we wanted out of sheer anticipation that it was possible? Conversely, how many times have we cut ourselves off at the pass by paying too much attention to possible obstacles?

Speaking up to get what you want, making contacts, aggressively seeking out means to facilitate meeting your ends, taking action without having to be prodded, putting a plan into motion, and enlisting others in your crusade all stem from one thing: initiative—which makes it a tremendously powerful personal resource. Approaching your goals and plans with "good attitude" means approaching them with positive expectations, a lot of initiative, a wide-angled imagination, and self-confidence. A good attitude is by far the best resource you can have coming out of the starting gates of all the races you run.

Resourceful Stories

When we pored over our notes and transcripts from talks and seminars to find a case that best illustrates as many of the types of resources (the Six P's) we've talked about here, we stumbled upon Angela. We heard Angela's story at a talk we hosted on college and work force reentry. While working as an assistant in a chiropractor's office, Angela became very involved with the patients—their injuries and ailments, their therapy, and their progress. She loved her work so much that she decided to look into physical therapy programs at local colleges and see if she could enroll. After looking at a few different programs, she visited the admissions counselors and financial aid officers at each school to find out about enrollment requirements and financial assistance.

Each college asked for high school and previous college transcripts and SAT scores, as well as income information. Having never before attended college, or taken the SAT exams, her work was cut out for her. Angela went to her public library and checked out a study manual for the SAT. In the meantime she filled out forms for financial aid, as well as visited each of the college's libraries to research grant and scholarship opportunities. She studied for the SAT exam every night and weekend until she felt pretty confident as to what to expect. She brushed up on various subjects and went to the tutor center at the YMCA to get help in math. Finally, she took the test and, four weeks later, got the results in the mail: she scored high enough to apply to all of the schools.

When she told the doctor she worked for of her plans, he was totally supportive. He even volunteered to assist her with her tuition and promised her an internship as a physical therapist when she completed her course of study. He even helped her arrange a flexible part-time schedule so she could keep her job as assistant in his office while going to school. Every so often he would give her trade literature on chiropractics and physical therapy.

Having been accepted at the college that offered the most financial aid, she was ready to start college. Her parents supported her plans and allowed her to move back home without paying rent. Even the patients who visited the office offered their support by volunteering to help her in any way they could. Throughout her planning to get into a physical therapy program, she confided in and sought the advice of her best friend. When she was feeling some hesitation about her age— that she wouldn't be finished with her program until she was thirty-three—her friend said, "Well, you're going to be thirty-three anyway, right? You might as well have something to show for it!"

Resourceful Questions

We'd like to stop for a moment now and ask you some questions. Try to be as comprehensive in your answers as you can and jot them down on a piece of paper.

- When you think of resources, what are the first ones that come to mind?
- What do you consider to be your personal resources? List them in order of importance.
- What resources outside of you do you use? List in order of importance.
- In the course of a typical day, what resources do you rely on?
- How have you used resources to get where you are? What were they?
- What resources could you use to help you reach your goals?
- How can resources help you fulfill your life plan? What ones would they be?
- What is the most creative or unique resource you've ever used to help you get what you want?
- What do you consider to be the one most important resource in your life? Why?
- Name one immediate goal in your life and what resources do you, could you, use to help you obtain it?

Take a minute to look at your answers. Take another minute to draft a resource list that you can use in your life. Include friends, coworkers, relevant family members (immediate and distant), contacts you have made over the years, old professors and bosses, people who might know someone else who could benefit you, organizations, libraries, schools, volunteer groups, and any other resource that may be of assistance. Your list should be tailor-made to suit the curves and specific needs of your life. Avoid adding resources that are not applicable to you so as not to dilute the significance or usefulness of your list.

Final Thoughts

Few people have ever accomplished what they want solely on their own. We realize that we have stressed self-reliance to a great extent in preceding chapters—"If It Is To Be, It Is Up To Me"—which is something we stand behind. It is up to you to get what you want out of your life. Resources are important and have value because they can help you get what you want. And in the final analysis, how you choose them, seek them out, and use them is solely up to you. Many of us were raised to not rely on others in any way, shape, or form—as if it were a matter of pride. That same thinking is reinforced by the value our culture places on personal privacy.

If this book is about any one thing, it is about helping you to arrange and think about your life in a way that is most rewarding and fulfilling to you. We are not, or will not, pretend that we know the secret to your personal fulfillment—there is no recipe or patented steps for that. We are saying, however, that happiness is your own journey. Fulfillment comes in many shapes and sizes, and it is up to you to recognize the dimensions that fit you. We are here to try to help you determine your own personal measurements. And in doing so, we implore you to use all the resources that are available to assist you in the very personal process of getting what you aim for in your life.

Chapter Seven

Aim to Make a Difference

The quality of a person's life is in direct proportion to their commitment to excellence, regardless of their chosen field of endeavor.

— *Vincent Lombardi*

When you say, "He is really special," or "She is really great at what she does," what is it about the people you're describing that makes you single them out? It is most likely because of the extra something that they give to whatever it is they do. Whether it is the CEO who cares enough to stop and say "Hello," or the friend who calls to see if you need anything when you're not feeling well, or the mechanic who checks your belts, hoses, and spark plugs when you get an oil change because he cares about your safety, they all have one thing in common—they aim to make a difference. The single most important thing we can do in our personal and professional lives to make ourselves remarkable is to put that extra touch on what we do.

In going the extra measure in how we do things, we demonstrate a variety of qualities. Besides commitment and conscientiousness, the most important thing our extra effort does is puts out a clear message that we care—not only about what we are doing, but about those who benefit from our extra touches. People love being around people who care, pure and simple.

Why does it make us feel good when someone does something as simple as holding a door open for us? Surely, it's something we can manage on our own. It's not the act that matters as much as it is the gesture of caring—that someone noticed we were there.

There are many doors we can hold open for others and, in doing so, make ourselves stand out as very special people. We dedicate this chapter to some of the very special people we've had the fortune to meet during our talks and travels, and we hope that their stories inspire you as much as they've inspired us.

The Golden Rule

Nancy is the president of a wholesale clothing company. When we asked her to tell us the most important factor in her success, she modestly replied, "I guess besides being effective in what I do, I've made it a rule to treat everyone with the same decency I would like to be treated with." When we probed a little to find out what decency meant to Nancy, she said, "It means treating people like human beings—with equality, fairness, kindness, and respect. You don't talk to a handyman or a secretary as if you were a better person because you're not. I guess that means you have to understand what equality is really all about. It's not just a policy someone wrote in a handbook, it's the way it is—and you have to live it.

"If you have to lay off someone, you not only give them notice, you give them an explanation. And you never do it unless it's an absolute last resort and never before the holidays! To avoid layoffs in the past, I ordered everyone to recycle everything from paper clips to typewriters, and prohibited all but absolutely essential executive travel! I have to give my company credit for appreciating how I do things. It obviously respects my respect for individuals. It could easily have chosen someone else to run the ship."

Suggest, Don't Complain

An assistant vice president for a large electronics retailer, Ron attributes every promotion he's ever received to one thing: doing everything that he's ever been asked to do with a smile—not one complaint. "By being the person people could count on, more and more people have wanted to count on me. I also have made it a habit to never bad-mouth anyone, especially my company. If I ever have a grievance, I turn it into something constructive in the form of a suggestion and send it through the appropriate channels. The only thing complaining does is slow down the works, makes you look bad, and creates bad energy—never do it!"

If Not You, Who?

When taking the subway home from downtown Manhattan one night last winter, we saw two young women serving hot soup to homeless people. Wanting to make a contribution to their effort, we asked them what organization was behind their charitable effort. When they told us that they did it on their own—that it was something they do every Friday night—we asked them what motivated them. "Well," one of the women responded, "I don't mean to be rude, but it's pretty obvious that these people need hot soup." Taken aback by her honest, direct reply, we gave them $20 and went through the turnstile to await the train. We were silent with amazement over how these two people decided to take it upon themselves to make the world a better place.

It's the Little Things That Count

You can often make a difference by the little things you do. At a seminar we hosted in Sacramento, California, a newspaper publisher described how he started out in newspapers as a copy boy—the one who would run errands, retrieve clip files from the library for reporters, make coffee, tear bulletins from the teletype machines, retrieve photos from the photo wires, and anything else that was needed to keep the newsroom running smoothly. Once when the teletype machine was broken, he decided to fix it himself. Not only did his repair work speed up the process of news getting to reporters, it also saved the paper a considerable expense. From then on, he fixed all the newsroom equipment, including the photo machines and typewriters—an extra touch that clearly benefited everyone and made him special in what he brought to his job.

There's a woman who works at the Burger King near where we work in midtown Manhattan who has such a pleasant manner that we often go out of our way to meet there for coffee. She's one of those very special people who have a gift for making you feel good. She always calls us by our first names, asks how we are, what's new in our lives, and asks if everything's been okay if she hasn't seen us for a while. With all the fancy restaurants in the area, Burger King is one of our favorite spots because she makes us feel like human beings—not customers. Her personal touch makes living in a very impersonal city a much nicer experience.

Measure by Extra Measure

Go out on a limb—that's where the fruit is.
—Anonymous

If you do not feel as if you are going the extra measure, start now and see what happens. We believe that your extra effort will not only make you feel better, it also will make you shine. So often when we see people put that added something into the things they do we think that it comes naturally to them—that it's a totally unconscious process. Well, we have no real way of knowing whether that's true or not, but we do know that we can all stand out in some way by making a conscious effort to do so.

Beyond Just Getting By

The biggest obstacle to becoming an outstanding player is attitude. A lot of people, sadly, have settled for just getting by—in their jobs and their lives. And although we live in a world that is filled with hardship, where just getting by can seem like a remarkable accomplishment, we think it's a self-imposed limit. After all, you have one chance to make the most of your life and this is it! You have to get rid of the get-by mind-set or that may be all you ever do—if that! If it's cynicism that is behind your get-by thinking, cheer up! If it's complacency, wake up! Whatever it is, convert your get-by outlook to a get-ahead one and look the rest of your life straight in the eye!

Don't Always Go by the Book

Sometimes making a difference means doing things differently—your way! If, for example, there's a better way to do something than a handed-down procedure tells you, then do it the better way! We're a nation of inventors and innovators—invent! Innovate! Don't do something differently for the sake of being different, however, but only if the difference counts—if it makes something better!

A bank manager who attended one of our talks told how she frequently strays from bank policy to do her job better. "It's not so much breaking the rules, but finding a way around them if they don't work or if they hinder the process of good business. One day a man came in who wanted to open an account but would only deal with the manager, which was me. I asked him into my office and he proceeded to tell me his story.

He had just moved to New York and had opened a new bank account at another New York bank, but the bank wouldn't release any funds to him until they received a signature verification from his old bank in California. Since this was before facsimile machines, the representative told him it would take a week to ten days to get the verification back from California. Until then he couldn't write checks against the $9,000 cashier's check he had deposited.

After three weeks he began to write checks against his money and they were all returned with a charge because the bank had not received the signature verification and still wouldn't release any funds. Enraged by the returned checks, he went to the bank and insisted upon seeing the manager. The manager explained that it was a matter of policy and there was nothing he could do about it and suggested that he "just be patient." The man was so furious, he demanded that the manager close his "useless" account and issue him a check for the money he had deposited. The manager cooperated but warned him that he would run into the same policy at any other bank. To that, the man replied, "I'll take my chances!"

The manager who told us this story said she was so outraged over the man's inconvenience that she got on the phone to his bank in California right then and there. She had asked him all his relevant personal information and did a personal information verification over the phone, and asked the bank to put a Xerox of his signature card in the mail that day. When she got off the phone, she smiled at the man and said, "That's that! You can write a check today—welcome to Republic National."

A Matter of Means and Ends

In theory the bank manager broke the rules—it really was policy to wait for a signature verification by mail before allowing funds to be released. But in practice she did her job better by securing and satisfying a new customer. We heard a similar rule-breaking story from a friend of ours who is a social worker—yes, the same social worker who wanted to go to law school. He told us how he often bends the rules when they keep him from doing his job as effectively as possible.

A general assistance case worker, our friend is well versed in attending to people's needs. In his case those needs often translate into a single mother and her four children who, by the end of the month, might be two cans of baked beans away from being hungry. People in such dire circumstances do not have the luxury to not mind if their welfare check is late. Because the welfare department, like any other government agency, is riddled with red tape, there are often reasons why checks are late.

"There are many times when my clients call and tell me that their check didn't come and that they need their money, food stamps, or medical stickers. After looking into the reason for the delay, and finding out it is our fault, I find a way to get the check issued that day. I often keep it on my desk and make sure it goes from my hand to theirs—something I'm not really supposed to do, but I do anyway because I am a social worker, not a bureaucrat."

The Hidden Agenda

In some professions, where rules aren't very flexible, the only way you can really make a difference in what you do is by keeping a hidden agenda. We were told the story of a New

York City public school teacher who was totally frustrated with how the curriculum she had to follow wasn't working very well with her fifth graders. As a teacher who had real passion for teaching, she decided she must do more than teach prescribed subjects from a prescribed approach.

Gradually, she started putting her own touches on the curriculum she was handed. Instead of teaching factors and prime numbers from the math textbook, she invented math games—which the students went wild over. After three factor games every student understood factors—something that they had struggled with for two months from the book. She did the same thing with all the subjects. She taught history from board games, and science from live experiments. Reading consisted of going to the library and having students pick out books of their own choice. Writing involved writing poetry and stories and keeping a journal, not essays on what you did last year or want to do next year.

Instead of making learning an uninspiring and repetitious chore, she brought it to life in ways that were relevant and exciting. In short, she made learning accessible to her students' experience. In order to teach children effectively, she had to write her own agenda. She followed the prescribed agenda just enough so she could say she did if anyone should ask. Her class, by the way, scored the highest marks on the Regents' exams of any other fifth grade class in her entire school district! She stands out as a model teacher to students, parents, and school administrators, even though no one knows exactly why!

Risk, Risk, Risk!

More often than not, making a difference means taking the necessary risks to be different, as in the stories we just shared with you. All these people took the initiative to do what they thought they had to do to do their jobs as effectively as possible. In taking the initiative, they also took risks—calculated ones. Rules are not arbitrary, and in these cases, each risked being reprimanded or, worse, fired. They thought about their actions, weighed action against consequence, and used their best judgment as to what should be done. They decided that the consequences of their actions were more beneficial than the consequences of following procedure—and, too, that asking for forgiveness is easier than asking for permission.

Risk Inhibition

It's often that moment of being totally alone in making a decision and taking action that people dread. They fear ever having to be accountable for their actions, and feel much more comfortable when they can point to a rule or another person. That's why obedience and conformity are such popular determinants of behavior. The problem with that, however, is twofold: one is the assumption that you're going to mess up or make the wrong decision, and two is that you never allow yourself the chance to make the right decision or take full credit for your accomplishments.

In learning how to take risks, you have to believe that you are doing the right thing. Think, weigh options, imagine possible consequences, think again, judge, decide, and either act or don't act. If you don't think you have enough information or knowledge to make the right decision, acknowledge that limitation and don't act. If, on the other hand, you think you can make an informed decision, act! Some of the best contributions in every human arena—small and big—have been made by taking informed risks. Informed risking is decision making; uninformed risking is gambling, which we don't often advocate.

Besides the risk of making the wrong decision, there are other risks involved in risk taking. Everyone laughed at Christopher Columbus when he said the world was round, and Abraham Lincoln risked his life when he declared the equality of all men in his address to a divided nation at Gettysburg. The risk we fear most in taking risks is loss—whether it be a job, money, family, personal growth, career growth, self-esteem, prestige, popularity, or a sense of safety or comfort with something familiar. At career-advancement seminars the most popular reason people give for not taking risks is the fear of losing a current job.

A woman recently told us that she felt jittery for six months after being promoted from sales manager to district sales manager at a beverage company. She tortured herself with unrelenting self-doubt: "What if I fail?" "What will I do if I get fired?" "How can I bow out now and get my old job back?" She managed to turn a wonderful promotion into a nightmare! The only thing that made it better, she said, was time. "The more time that went by, the less afraid I was of not passing some hidden scrutiny that I was sure was taking place. Six months was the turning point because that's the probation period for all hires and promotions at my company. I don't think I could ever put myself through anything like that again!"

Don't Put a Lid on Your Thinking

In order to take risks while aiming to make a difference, you have to take the lid off your thinking. Instead of locking yourself into a particular way of doing things, even if it is your company's usual practice or procedure, try to open yourself up to different possibilities. Don't be so loyal to established routines that you cut yourself off from your own creativity. Not only can your way of doing something be more efficient, it can also be a source of enjoyment, growth, and renewal. Wallace Stevens wrote a poem called "Thirteen Ways of Looking at a Blackbird," meaning that there's often more than one way of seeing something. The same is true about how we do things. There might not always be thirteen ways of doing something, but we guarantee there's more than one! Open your eyes! Unleash the creator and make a difference!

In practically all the stories we've brought you in this chapter, each of the main players was open to more than just the handed-down ways of doing things. Nancy, the president of a wholesale clothing company, didn't automatically lower the axe when she got the word to trim the staff. She looked at options and decided to trim company expenses instead. She was not fired, she was applauded. Not only was her concern for individuals the right thing, it also made her company a better company. By taking the lid off her thinking, the teacher we mentioned strayed from the established curriculum that wasn't working and developed one that did. And not content to wait for the large and far-reaching solution that was out of their hands, the women who made soup for the homeless figured out their own way to ease one small part of the misery in the world.

Final Thoughts

As we said earlier, reality is born in the imagination. If you can think something, it's probably possible. If you can't or don't, it probably won't be. In aiming to make a difference in what you do, you have to believe that you can make a difference and to believe it, you have to imagine it! Whatever form that difference may come in, and in whatever arena it will be expressed, can only be determined by you. Where you put your energy to make a difference will depend on where you know best to put it. The only thing we can suggest to you is to let your heart be your guide.

People tend to gravitate toward their passions—the things they love. And the difference they make in what they do or how they do it most certainly must come out of that love—that passion, that caring. Making a difference, like most things that matter, is not an arbitrary process—you can't choose just anything. It has to involve some real part of who you are—your interests, your knowledge, your talents, your understanding of people or the world. It is like finding the things that make you tick—not just anything makes you tick.

The same is true for the goals we choose. We are most successful at reaching goals that are important to us, that we have passion for, that we care about reaching. If we set a goal to become a gardener but have no interest in gardening, that goal, like so many others, will probably end up in the huge unfulfilled goal heap that people have been adding to since the beginning of time. If you have a knack for computers, express it in how you use them. If you have a great love for others, direct your energy toward people and, in so doing, make the world a better place. Any extra measure that you can take to make a difference in the world or in what you do will come from one place and one place only—those things that matter most to you, that *are* most you.

PART III

YOU AT WORK

Man, unlike any other thing organic or inorganic in the universe, grows beyond his work, walks up the stairs of his concepts, emerges ahead of his accomplishments.

—*John Steinbeck*

We are living in hard times. More and more, people are looking at what they do for a living as making a living, not as a life. We have encouraged you throughout this journey not to define yourself solely from your job role. Yet it is an undeniable fact that we spend a good deal of our lives working. Because we do, we should always aim to get as much satisfaction from our jobs as we can. When we are not able to feel satisfied in our jobs, we must stretch ourselves to find fulfillment elsewhere, as well as in different ways of finding it in our jobs.

Changing jobs is not always possible, especially when the job market is as tenuous as it is now. Instead of feeling limited by the condition of the times, we can turn it into a source of growth and expansion. We are presented with the challenge of having to come up with creative ways to meet our desire for job fulfillment. Sometimes changing jobs or advancing in our jobs will be the best route to satisfaction, and we must prepare ourselves to make that happen. When opportunity knocks, we have to open the door.

Freud said that we all need to love and work to be healthy. We think so, too. As the expansive beings we are, we will never be happy keeping our minds on just one thing. We will always look for balance from a variety of activities and interests. A job is one of those activities, one interest. It has the potential to give us some of our satisfaction, but only in proportion to what we bring to it. How we approach our jobs as one of our many sources of personal fulfillment is the journey we will now take.

Chapter Eight
_____

Does Your Job Pass Your Test?

For those of us who work traditional nine-to-five jobs, every workday morning bears a similar scene: We wake up, take a shower, get dressed, have breakfast, read the paper, and head off to our jobs. Our rituals ground us and lend us a sense of certainty as we prepare ourselves to be measured by our day's work. At our jobs our work is under constant scrutiny. Performance evaluations, remarks and certain looks from our bosses and peers, written reports, bonuses or lack of bonuses, and other more or less subtle forms of review all serve at all times to measure us. Unendingly, we are put to the test.

How often, however, do we turn the table around and put our jobs to the test? When was the last time you took a long moment to reflect and ask yourself whether your job meets your standards? Well, that's what we want you to do now. Your job may pass with flying colors, fail miserably, or, most likely, will fall in the middle somewhere. Whatever the outcome is, what you learn is important information that can help you maximize the satisfaction you receive from what you spend so much of your precious life's time doing.

The average person works at least forty years of his or her adult life. After subtracting weekends, holidays, and two weeks of vacation a year, we spend about ten thousand days at work.

Based on an eight-hour day (and no overtime), that means we punch more than nine straight years of our lives into a time clock. At one time forty years was our whole life expectancy— now it is our work life expectancy. For any one thing to demand so much of us, it should provide us with more than a means to a livelihood.

What Makes You Tick Revisited

In taking that long moment to evaluate what your job does and doesn't do for you, it's important to get back to the very same question we asked at the beginning of this journey: What makes you tick? More specifically, what makes you tick at work? What do you enjoy most about what you do on the job? What gives you satisfaction? What specific things come to mind when you think about why you have the job you have? Does the shoe fit, kind of fit, or does it not fit at all? Will a shoehorn help, or how about a shoe tree? Do you have the right job but the wrong place? Or, perhaps, the right place but the wrong job?

Don't get nervous, we're not going to ask you to change jobs. In fact, we're going to ask something quite the opposite, as in "Is there a way you can be happier with your job?" Many people change jobs for the wrong reasons. They might be unhappy, bored, or just going through a sea change and, automatically, they grab at a quick solution—change jobs, get divorced, relocate, or whatever else might represent a speedy ticket out of their current circumstance. We think a more realistic, lasting, and less traumatic way to approach unease is by working within whatever circumstances may be bringing you down. Changing jobs is often an impulsive attempt at finding a quick solution.

No Patience for Process

We are so enamored by instant results and gratification that we have no patience for process. When we decide we don't like the color of a particular shirt anymore, we throw it out and buy a new one. What about dyeing the old one? We don't usually want to bother. Part of the reason is our consumer orientation. Instead of fixing things, we discard them and buy new ones. And that same orientation has flowed over into other areas of our lives—including our jobs.

The vast majority recognizes that our jobs are not disposable, however. And as much as we sometimes wish we could change jobs, it's not always possible, especially when the job market is as tenuous as it is now. More important, however, is that we don't always have to. With a little process, we can derive more satisfaction from our jobs than we might have thought possible. At this point we want you to get a pen and paper, sit down, get comfortable, and begin to look closely at your current satisfaction level at work. Jot down any ideas that come to you.

Reading the Satisfaction Barometer

In determining your current job satisfaction, try to concentrate on subjective indicators such as interest, enjoyment, a sense of meaning, challenge, and how you feel about yourself while performing your job. In short, look at job content—the actual tasks involved in your job and the feeling performing them gives you.

If you are a human resources director, for example, what satisfaction do you derive from your actual job functions? Perhaps you are good at creating employment policies, and that's why you do what you do. But, in reality, you have a very small hand in determining your company's policies—they are handed down by higher-ups—a condition that limits your job satisfaction. Your job consists primarily of directing correspondence that concerns your company's policies, which makes you feel like a paper shuffler and that your best skills are not being called upon. Should you quit your job, look for a job elsewhere, become an independent consultant, approach your superiors with your concern, or should you try to highlight what you do enjoy about your current employment despite its limitations?

We suggest first approaching your superiors in a nonthreatening way. Set up a meeting to discuss an idea or ideas you have that might enrich the current policy at your company. Don't voice your dissatisfaction in any way, shape, or form— go into it strictly as a contributor. This way no hairs are raised and you come across as a conscientious and involved player who wants to go the extra measure—all valued attributes that will earn you good marks. Get a solid read on the feedback at the meeting. If it looks as if the door is open, be patient and follow up the meeting in a week or so to see where things stand. If it looks as if the door is locked, go to Plan B.

Plan B is to evaluate your job further. Start by listing all the things you like and dislike about your day-to-day job role. If the plus column is longer than the minus column, try to focus on the things you enjoy and tune out your dislikes as much as possible. By tuning out, we mean defocusing—doing the less enjoyable parts of your job by rote and keeping your attention primarily for those things from which you derive satisfaction, stimulation, and enjoyment.

If the negatives outweigh the positives, see if there's a way you can shift the tide. If possible, spend more time on what you enjoy and less time on what you don't. Try to think pleasant thoughts while performing the least satisfying parts of your job as a way to help get you through them. Visualize people, places, and activities that bring you joy. At those times think of your job as a means to an end. Be creative—try out different strategies! If you find nothing works, then you're ready for Plan C—thinking seriously about options that exist outside your current employment situation.

Creative Solutions

Joan, a woman we met at a seminar in Chicago, told about her strategy for making an unpleasant part of her job more tolerable. A writer for a large corporation, Joan loves her job ten months out of the year but dreads it the other two—when she works on her company's annual report. For the first two years at her company, writing the annual report made Joan so miserable that she wanted to quit.

She was very conflicted, however, because she enjoyed everything else about her job. After getting through the second annual report, she decided she had to do something to prevent it from being as unbearable the next year. At first she thought of lining up a new job in the next ten months, but that made her feel very stressed and uncertain about her life. She decided, instead, to try to come up with a solution without escaping.

After looking at her options (which weren't many), she thought maybe if she took a few days off before writing the annual report and a vacation afterward, she would prepare herself with relaxation and reward herself with something really pleasurable. Thinking that she had nothing to lose, she put her plan into motion. She put in for the time off way in advance and booked a week-long trip to a ski resort north of Montreal. When oppressive October approached, she felt like a different person—her solution was already having a positive effect!

Not only did she no longer live in dread over the annual report time of year, she looked forward to it as the same time of year she'd take her vacation! And when the time actually came, the two months passed more quickly because her vacation was nearing. Whenever she got bummed out by her tedious project, she fantasized about what she'd do on her vacation. Also, the few days' rest she took before beginning the project gave her added energy and a better frame of mind to approach it with. Since then, she has glided through four more annual reports!

Choice Versus Circumstance

Often we have jobs that are not our dream jobs. And we don't always have the luxury to choose what we do for a living. "Do for a living" is exactly what most jobs are—a means to a livelihood. The expression isn't what we "do for fun, excitement, growth, challenge, or personal or spiritual satisfaction." "Do for a living" is an expression passed down to us from years and years of observation—people have always worked as a way to provide for necessities of living. Some of us are fortunate enough to have had the education and opportunities to have jobs that are personally rewarding and interesting, while many of us have had to accept what we could get and make the most of it.

Make the Most Out of What You've Got

The real challenge that faces all of us—no matter what job we have—is to make the most out of what we have. We're not advocating coming to terms with your misery if you can do something else, but we do want to be realists. So often the advice people proffer isn't as simple as they make it sound. Changing jobs, like any big life change, can create a tremendous amount of upheaval and, sometimes, unnecessary hardship. We think there is a way to come to terms with imperfect jobs and find ways to make them more satisfying.

Satisfaction, like any perception, is an interpretation. An experience is satisfying or not satisfying depending on how we look at it. Some experiences are clearly more enjoyable than others, but many are vague. For those more ambiguous ones, try to lean toward whatever positives you can find. Often we are made miserable by miserable perceptions. When we open our minds, we also open our lives. We have to start by giving up our quest for perfection. Nobody has the perfect job or the perfect anything else! Unless you relax your definition of satisfaction, your interpretations of it will be pretty strict and rigid. Loosen up and see if you can find joy in uncommon places.

The Elusive Greener Pasture

A friend of ours has been looking for greener pastures for twenty years and he still hasn't found them. He started out in advertising and ended up hating the industry in less than two years. He jumped into publishing, and lasted nearly three years. In desperation, he tried out for the police force, thinking it was excitement that was lacking, but had second thoughts before going into the academy. He took a job as a claims adjuster for a large insurance agency, which gave him the opportunity to get out of the confines of an office five days a week (a big gripe he had about his other jobs), but even that wasn't enough. Again and again we asked him what it was he was looking for, what he wanted, but he was never quite able to say.

For the time being our friend is an accounts manager in the credit department of a large retail clothing store, a job he's had for four years. Already he is restless and wants something else, but still is not focused about what "that" might be. After the first ten years of this kind of behavior, we kind of got the message that he wasn't able to be happy doing anything. He just didn't have it in him to enjoy what he does for a living.

Sensing this, we approached him with it. "Jim, have you ever stopped to think that maybe your jobs aren't going to give you the happiness you want from them? Is there some way that you can just accept that and quit beating yourself up? Maybe your happiness will come from some other aspect of your life!" He took our words in, but still is looking for his professional utopia.

People Who Turn it Around

In the last chapter we mentioned quite a few very special people who managed to get more from their jobs by stretching the rules a bit. The social worker who found a way through the red tape, the teacher who created her own agenda, and the president of the wholesale clothing company who let her ethics guide her decisions not only made a difference, but all received more satisfaction from their jobs than if they had gone strictly by the book. We don't advocate breaking the rules if you don't have to, but we do recommend stretching them if they are strangling your sense of satisfaction!

Employers Are Pitching In, Too

Many employers have recognized the American work force's quest for fulfillment from their jobs and have responded with a variety of employment policies that value their aim. Carol Kinsey Goman's book, *The Loyalty Factor* (MasterMedia, 1991), lists many companies that have enacted "quality-of-worklife" programs as a means of keeping employees satisfied. The author says W. L. Gore & Associates, the highly successful maker of Gore-Tex and other products, was founded on the philosophy: "To get rich and have fun." Many companies today have employee-involvement programs, and are experimenting in involving employees in day-to-day decisions. When you feel as if you are up against a brick wall as far as your happiness at work goes, see if your employer can help you find a creative solution.

Our Search for Meaning

Sometimes it's not so much a matter of lack of satisfaction from our jobs as it is lack of meaning. We stumbled upon the issue of job meaning at a talk we gave on goals. In a group discussion an accountant said his goal was to make some sort of contribution to the world. He said he liked his job, the people he worked with, and felt that he has made significant contributions to his company, but that something was missing. He wasn't quite sure what his goal should be, but he knew he needed one. In the course of the discussion, someone suggested that he volunteer to keep the books at a nonprofit organization that he cared about. Suddenly, his face lit up, as if something had just struck home.

About three months later we received a note from the accountant thanking us for having invited him to the goal session, and added, "Something clicked for me—that my job was not the only means by which to make my mark in the world. I now volunteer my time keeping accounts for a pediatrics clinic in my city. With your inspiration, I found a goal worth working for, and now my life seems to matter more. You were right, too, about not always being able to find all your joy in one place. I'm no longer blaming my company for not giving me what I had to find for myself."

Your Job Is Not the Only You

Throughout this journey we have cautioned against letting your job or any other one thing dominate your identity. A job is just a job, and although it plays a very important role in our lives, it does not by any means constitute our lives or who we are. We often fall into the trap of relying on our jobs for too much—a livelihood, personal satisfaction, stimulation, challenge, and a catalyst for growth. And although it would be wonderful if our jobs or any other part of our lives could meet so many needs, it is unlikely.

Besides unlikely, it's unrealistic. You have to ask yourself if you are expecting too much from your job. Are you, in some way, making your job unrealistically responsible for your fulfillment? Are you spending your free time to your best advantage—time, perhaps, that you could direct to a talent or interest or concern from which you could derive some of your sense of fulfillment? Are you getting joy from a variety of places? Are you getting a share of your satisfaction at home? Or are you putting the onus on your job to be and do all things? If you are, your assessment of it may be skewed. Before you leap to a negative pronouncement of what you do for a living, make sure you are doing enough living!

Back to the Beginning

So, where are you? With all things considered, how would you measure your job? It was important to go full circle to help you begin to see some of the hidden reasons you may not be feeling as much satisfaction from your job as you would like. So many books are quick to tell you that change is the answer to everything. We don't think it is. Sometimes the real challenge is to see what is good and satisfying in what you have, including your job, and not be so quick to trade it in for something else. That's not to say that you might have indeed looked for the good and couldn't find it. That happens. And if that's the case with your job, then it's time to evaluate it while keeping an open mind to the best, least intrusive kind of change that is available to you.

Whether or not you are satisfied with your job, we'd like you to stop now and answer some questions. Jot down your answers on a piece of paper as well as any other enlightening thoughts that occur to you.

- What do you like most about your job?
- What do you like least about your job?
- What strategies could you use to minimize what you dislike?
- Is there a way you can spend more time doing what you like?
- Does your job challenge your skills or knowledge?
- Does your job challenge your growth?
- What other things in your life challenge your growth?
- Do you feel good about going to work?
- Do you feel reasonably satisfied at the end of a work week?
- List all the sources in your life you derive satisfaction from.
- Do you feel good about your future?
- Do you think you get paid enough for what you do?
- Could you earn more money for the same work elsewhere?
- Do you have unrealistic expectations about your job?
- Would more education or training help you enjoy your job more?
- Does your employer offer tuition reimbursement?
- Can your employer help you increase your job satisfaction?
- When was the last time you updated your résumé to see your skills in process?
- Have you formed a network of contacts at your company?

Final Thoughts

If you get up most mornings truly looking forward to the day's activities, and if you end most days with a sense of accomplishment, then you have a very satisfying job. You are among the fortunate few whose work days provide them with a feeling of purpose and gratification in addition to giving them the means by which they can pay their bills. If, however, you are like the vast majority, you have a fair amount of gripes mixed in with your joys. If your job is truly life draining, and gives you nothing but a means to pay the bills, you are among the desperate minority who absolutely should change jobs.

We thought very hard about what to bring you in this chapter. The truth is, we were very tempted to take the easy route and give you a pep talk about how you should change jobs if your job doesn't meet your satisfaction standards. But after much discussion we weren't convinced that change is the best route. One reason is that change is not always harmonious, even though it appeals to the fantasy in each of us to make something better instantly.

The main reason we decided not to advocate changing jobs, though, is because change isn't always the best solution. Our tendency to want quick solutions makes change very alluring, but often learning how to accept process is a more lasting solution. Being able to work through something is certainly less consuming than starting from scratch—whether it is a job, a marriage, or a life crisis. Using our imaginations and creativity to make the most out of what we have is a far more economical use of our life's time than is whiling it away searching for the perfect job or the perfect anything else.

The evaluations we make of our jobs are important mainly as a means to keep us vigilant at being aware of what makes us happy. Our standards, whether they're ever met wholly or not, are our measuring sticks for life. We should never be content when our lives don't measure up to the values we hold dear to us, including what we want from our jobs. But we must be aware that we play a very active role in the much-talked-about job satisfaction factor. We are not passive recipients of satisfaction, we play a big part in creating it! Our evaluations of our jobs are are also evaluations of ourselves. We have to probe not only what our jobs bring to us, but what we bring to our jobs. More important, we must ask, what can we bring to our jobs to help them bring more to us?

Chapter Nine

The Art of Networking and Self-Promotion

At a recent talk we gave on networking, a woman in the audience asked, "Isn't networking yesterday's news?" It might be yesterday's news, we answered, but it's today's reality! In the 1980s networking was a pipeline, in the 1990s it's a lifeline. In the midst of a dismal economy and widespread company lay-offs, networking is no longer an option, it's a must. We don't mean networking in terms of just exchanging as many business cards as possible, but being and keeping "in the know." Being in the know means creating and keeping communication channels open in your job and the larger industry. It also means forming ongoing alliances with people you've known over the years—friends, family, college peers and professors, former coworkers and bosses, and members of organizations you belong to or once belonged to—the same people resources we talked about in chapter 6.

Research shows that about 75 percent of most successful attempts to find jobs or change jobs through "networking" are made indirectly—by someone you know putting the word out to someone they know who can help you or who may know somebody else who can. When people do get jobs from people they don't know—there is usually a known go-between. The reason for this is that networking—before it was called networking—has always been a very informal process, people helping out the people they know.

Nothing New Under the Sun

This tendency to "do favors" has always taken place among people in societies. People networked pretty inconspicuously through their extended families, friendships, sharing information about other families and their community, and keeping abreast of what was happening in the next community. In short, networking was the simple process of tapping into the pipeline of local information. Those most involved in their community were the most "in the know" and had the most extensive networks. Those least involved had the smallest networks.

It is important that you view networking as keeping an open line of communication. The art of networking is really the art of keeping the line open—not ever fading out of contact with others. If you are out of contact, get back in! Sometimes the telephone feels as if it weighs fifty pounds! If that's the case, ease into it—a note out of the blue is appropriate. If that makes you feel uncomfortable, send a card during the holidays—a great time for renewing old acquaintances. Besides providing a solid support system—and joy—ongoing alliances with others can save a lot of time and money when it comes to searching for jobs, schools for your child, the best doctors, clubs, volunteer opportunities, or just about anything else.

Don't Be Afraid to Ask

Often people feel uncomfortable asking for things. Besides living in a culture that values privacy and self-reliance, some people are just too embarrassed or proud to let others know they need help. Some people are too shy. It's important to overcome all of these barriers if you want to be a good net-worker and, in some cases, a better provider. At one of our seminars, a young woman told the story about how her mother's pride affected her family's standard of living:

"My mom was a single mother of five children. She worked all the time and was always just barely making ends meet. When I was ten, she had a chance to be promoted from sales manager of a large department store to district sales manager— a move that translated to about $10,000 a year more! Although she applied for the new position, she didn't talk to anyone about it. She felt that it was wrong to ask outright for some-thing, that merit was its own reward, and if they wanted her to fill the spot, they would come to her! Needless to say, they never did." Performance is not always rewarded. It's the old story—"You don't ask, you don't get!"

Be Focused

Often people scatter themselves all over the place in their job-search efforts, and cut off their nose to spite their face. You need to be focused! The December 7, 1992, *Wall Street Journal* reported ("From Beltway to Boardroom"), "Prior to 'network-ing' with everyone you have ever met, narrow your focus to just a few industries. The more targeted you are the better people will be able to point you in the right direction."

Madeleine and Robert Swain, authors of *Out the Organiza-tion* (MasterMedia, 1992), reported that 95 percent of five hun-dred networked executives they surveyed agreed that "the most effective networking seems to result when the job cam-paign is clearly and specifically focused. Otherwise, effort spent in developing the network is wheel-spinning."

Spell it Out

Not only do you have to be focused, you have to articulate your desires clearly. If you come across as being clear and decisive about what you want, people will take your requests more seriously and try harder to fill them. You also have to be clear about letting others know how they can help you. Telling your boss that you want to be the systems analyst for your company, and that he or she can help you by teaching you all the nuances involved in the new software, is a very clear request about your aims and how he or she can help you. By enlisting people's help you not only give them a message of trust, you cause them to feel invested in your progress. You have communicated your goal effectively, and have personalized the whole process.

A recent seminar attendee told us that she finally got up enough nerve to ask an old acquaintance of hers—who just happened to be the vice president of a cosmetics company—out to lunch. Too embarrassed to ask for a job outright, the woman took special pains to talk as indirectly as she could about her strengths, the type of job she was looking for, and how she could contribute to that type of job. She even hinted as to how the VP could help her. As they finished their lunch, the VP asked, "So, how can I help you?" Our attendee was crushed! She had been so subtle that the VP had missed her request entirely!

Self-Promotion

If we were not all so excessively interested in ourselves, life would be so uninteresting that none of us would be able to endure it!

—*Arthur Schopenhauer*

The surest way to network successfully is through self-promotion. By positioning yourself at work as a highly visible and important player, you pave the way to advancement. What do the grand promoters such as Ross Perot, Donald Trump, and Madonna have in common? They are all experts in the art of self-promotion. Whether they are promoting an idea, an act, or a project, they know how to put the most into their messages and how to get the most out of them. In short, they are great communicators. They took the time to find out what their audiences expected and then attempted to deliver the goods.

Self-promotion doesn't have to be done on such a grand scale, however. In fact, it shouldn't be. The most effective self-promotion should be as invisible as possible so as not to come across as obnoxious or egomaniacal. To be effective, you should promote yourself subtly, but not too subtly—as we'll discuss later.

Often people equate "self-promotion" with self-aggrandizement and are automatically turned off. They think of the grand promoters like Madonna and Donald Trump. But the self-promotion we are talking about is along the lines of how you position yourself—accenting your positives, taking credit for your accomplishments, and reminding others that you are a contributor.

Taken to an extreme, self-promotion tends to have a negative effect by making you seem egocentric and desperate for recognition—traits that point to an underlying insecurity. Taken to the opposite extreme, you can undermine your efforts by underpromoting yourself. Being too subtle risks wasting your time and effort if no one gets your messages! You have to use good, balanced judgment and not second-guess yourself. If you are uncomfortable, start out slowly. Find opportunities to test your self-promotion skills. Feel out others' responses to your efforts and use that feedback to further hone your skills.

Try out a few different ways of promoting yourself, such as pointing out your contributions, taking credit for a good idea, or coming up with an innovative strategy. If there is no response, you're probably underpromoting, so increase your efforts. If your efforts come back to hit you in the face, you have probably gone too far. Try to chart a course that you can correct along the way.

Do Your Homework: Know Your Business

A great way to promote yourself is by knowing your business—the rules, regulations, organizational structure, plans, objectives, philosophies, projects in progress, inside information, financials, who's who, and all the miscellaneous whats and whys. Read the company handbook, directories, transcripts of the CEO's and president's speeches, annual reports, and anything else you can get your hands on.

Also be an expert in your field. Keep well informed about industry news and innovations, and seek out knowledge that makes you better at what you do. Your knowledge of your company and your profession is sure to dazzle others—incorporate it into your remarks and conversations without seeming conspicuous, and let it help guide your actions.

Identify Key Players

Step back and assess who it is that can make a difference in your career and get to know what their expectations are. Find out, specifically, what their expectations of you, your position, and future departmental growth are. Establish an open line of communication with those who can play a role in your advancement. We are not saying you should find a mentor. We would rather see you create many strategic alliances within your company than hitch your wagon to one star—which could turn out to be the wrong one! Concentrate on forming strategic alliances with customers, clients, supervisors, departmental directors, or other management personnel—depending on your position. You can find out what their expectations are by coming right out and asking them, asking others, observing them, and by learning their track records. You will save yourself time, energy, and a lot of guesswork if you learn up front what is expected of you.

Be Wary of Bright Lights

Don't confuse self-promotion with Hollywood—it has nothing to do with spotlights and brass bands. It is securing recognition from those individuals who will in some way be in a position to assist you in furthering your efforts to achieve your career goals.

We knew a man who thought he would gain recognition by being the first to arrive at the office and the last to leave. He made sure that he walked by the president's office every morning and every evening with the hope of being singled out for his hard work and dedication. Every time he was asked a question at a meeting, however, he gave hesitant answers. Finally, the president said to this man's boss, "Get rid of that guy. I've never seen anyone work so hard at getting nothing done! Let's get someone who works smarter, not harder."

You have to back up your self-promotion with performance. You can't just make campaign promises without delivering solid goods! There is no substitute for a job well done. The heart of effective self-promotion is calling attention to positive job performance. It lets people know who you are, what you've accomplished, and what you are capable of doing. It's the old "who, what, wow!"

Promotion Promises

The rule to follow is to promote to the point of promise. Call attention to what you know you can deliver or even a little bit beyond that point. Stretch yourself. Even make yourself feel as though you've overextended yourself in the promise you've made—and rise to meet a challenge! WHATEVER YOU DO, DON'T CALL ATTENTION TO YOURSELF IF YOU CANNOT DELIVER THE GOODS AS PROMISED! That's a cardinal sin in business, and people don't readily forget it. Reneging on a promise instantly destroys your credibility, as well as diminishes the meaning of your past positive performance.

Creating a Spotlight

A senior vice president of a financial services company attended a seminar we spoke at in New York City. She told of how she used self-promotion to catapult from one level to the next at her company. As a senior vice president, she reported directly to the president, which meant that there was no next level to catapult to unless she was content to wait in line for the top spot. Being the forward-mover that she was, waiting for an indeterminate time for an uncertain outcome was an unlikely option.

During her climb at her company, she had become an authority on her industry, but had never promoted herself as an expert outside of her corporation. She took the initiative and hired a public relations consultant, and also took a media training course. She promoted herself to television and radio stations, and was invited to appear on financial news features. She was also regularly quoted in the press. Her increased profile paid off—an industry headhunter started tracking her progress and within six months she was offered the top spot at a competitive financial services company.

A similar scenario—though with drastically different consequences—occurred with another one of our clients. Jim, a group product manager at a major pharmaceutical company, had received a call from a reporter who requested a quote or two about a new product introduction. Thinking that it would highlight his profile with the outside world, he consented to be interviewed. On the day the article came out, Jim received a call from the president's office reprimanding him for giving out proprietary information. It was company policy that only the public relations department could speak with the press! Instead of promoting himself, Jim was caught having not done his homework.

The Importance of Personal Presentation

Your personal presentation also plays a part in how effective you are in promoting yourself. Having the right physical presentation is key to how you position yourself to others. Research has revealed that when meeting someone, impressions are made within the first four to seven seconds! Before you've shaken hands, handed someone a résumé, or taken a seat at a meeting, someone has checked you out! In promoting yourself as a confident, competent, and capable team player, you have to look the part—credibility is intimately linked to presentation. We are a visually oriented society that puts much stock in images. We like to look a particular way, and we like others to also. We perceive image as a combination of confidence and self-esteem, clothing and style, and behavior, gestures, and actions.

We've all heard stories about people not being moved along because they didn't project the appropriate image. A publisher of a woman's magazine received a great résumé from a sales executive. Having called her in for an interview, the publisher had high expectations of the person she would meet. When the woman showed up for her interview dressed totally inappropriately and slovenly, the publisher nearly collapsed. She thought to herself, "If this woman can't even get it together for an interview, how in the world does she expect to run my ad department?!"

It is a well-known fact that corporate management hires and promotes in its own image. Whether the practice is right or wrong, it is a reality. The smart player recognizes the rules and plays by them.

Self-Promotion Scale

The first step in self-promotion is to assess where you're at on the self-promotion scale. Are you currently making yourself visible or are you working diligently behind the scenes? To see where you are, answer the following questions. Give yourself one point for each "yes."

- Do you feel comfortable tooting your own horn?
- Do you take credit for your work?
- Do you network within your company?
- Do you network outside your company?
- Have you ever reviewed your accomplishments with your boss?
- Do you offer sound input at meetings?
- Are you an artist at networking?
- Do you CC: key people in your memos?

- Do you maintain the right image?
- Do you know the dos and don'ts of your company?

Scoring:
0–3 = Stage 0
4–5 = Stage 1
6–8 = Stage 2
9–10 = Stage 3

If you are at Stage 0, you can consider yourself pretty much behind the scenes. Try to do at least four of the things on the test list to get a good start at making yourself visible at work. If you are at Stage 1, you are already making yourself visible. Try for more visibility by advancing to Stage 2. If you are at Stage 2, we predict that you've already experienced some job advancement by now. No one does that much promoting without results—keep up the good work! If you are at Stage 3, bravo! You are definitely of the same ilk as the grand promoters!

Getting Beyond Negative Thinking About Self-Promotion

Many people are uncomfortable with the whole notion of self-promotion. We've heard a range of comments, such as "I don't feel comfortable talking about myself," "I think it's obnoxious and egocentric," "If you're good at something, you don't have to advertise," "Merit is its own reward," "I'm too modest," and on and on. These kinds of comments didn't come out of a vacuum. The truth is, self-promotion goes against an ingrained social more that discourages us from making ourselves the center of attention. We value modesty and discourage egocentricism.

It is helpful if you approach self-promotion as a means to an end, not as the object of a value judgment. You are not self-promoting because it is your nature, you are doing it to advance your career! It's unfortunate that corporate management—in most cases—is still not people-oriented enough to take responsibility for recognizing peak performers. The onus, instead, falls on the performer. Employees are forced to publicize their accomplishments and capabilities if they want to advance with ease. So try not to think of yourself as the odd person out when you begin to promote yourself. Think of yourself, instead, as taking your future into your own hands.

Another genre of comments we've frequently heard reflects a different kind of obstacle. "My boss won't let me do anything extra," "I don't want to step on my boss' toes," "My boss takes credit for my work," "I don't want my boss to ice me out." Can you identify what word each of these comments has in common? Right—boss! Intimidation or harassment by a boss is a very real barrier to many people's comfort in promoting themselves. After all, your boss is your most immediate supervisor.

People ask, "If I alienate my boss by self-promoting, aren't I undermining myself?" The answer is "No!" If your boss is that insecure, that's all the more reason to move on and out from under his or her thumb! If your boss is taking credit for your good work, that's wrong! Boss-intimidation is just like any other form of intimidation—an oppressive and destructive force that should never be tolerated. If your boss is exerting such negative influence over you, a meeting with a higher-up is in order.

Gender Differences

Self-promoting is harder for women than men. A woman's socialization tells her from day one not to be aggressive, not to push herself out into the world, to be kind, soft-spoken, and nurturing. Men, on the other hand, have been encouraged to do just the opposite: Do whatever you must to get what you want—push, shove, shout, hit your fist on the table! It's only natural that men can promote themselves with greater ease than women.

For women to compensate for the greater discomfort they might feel in promoting themselves, we suggest that they arm themselves with the very awareness of the inequity. By knowing that some of the discomfort they feel has been imposed, we think they will try harder to fight it. Also, by anticipating the discomfort, they are better prepared to get beyond it and to not attribute the feeling to something in their nature.

Getting Started

To get you started on your self-promotion campaign, we've compiled some tips we've gathered from successful self-promoters:

- Keep a positive mental attitude—enthusiasm sells!
- Tell yourself you are valuable.
- Make sure your strategy is appropriate for your company.
- Don't overpromote.
- Don't underpromote.
- Look great!
- Do your homework.
- Take smart chances.
- Deliver the goods—don't break promises.
- Ask for feedback.
- Stretch yourself day-by-day.
- Remind yourself what your goals are.

Final Thoughts

When thinking about networking and self-promotion, we want you to focus on one thing: making yourself visible—how to increase your visibility, how to maintain it, and how to use it to get what you want. Remind everyone who is relevant to your professional life who you are, where you are, and what you can do. Renew contacts that you've left by the wayside and nurture the ones that are in your life now. Plant seeds to cultivate new contacts in the future. People can be a huge resource—introduce yourself!

Above all, don't get lost behind the scenes, and don't let your contributions go unnoticed or let others take credit for them. Be aggressive about speaking up to get what you want. Try to ignore old tapes that tell you such an attitude or behavior is wrong. Pushy people have been getting what they want from the dawn of time. If it's too hard to be aggressive outright, couch it in tact and diplomacy—let your wits do the pushing! Approach your job and your life with confidence, and tell yourself that you deserve whatever goals you pursue. Before you know it, others will pick up on the very same message and will be there to help you along. But don't take any chances, tell others exactly what it is that you want—and how they can help!

Chapter Ten

Winning Traits: What Goes into Making You Stand Out

We've all read or seen books that promise to enlighten us with the secret to success, how to make it in business, how to be a leader, how to raise a happy child, what goes into the perfect marriage, or, simply, how to be an effective person. What we have learned from our clients, however, is that success, happiness, and personal fulfillment rarely have single facets. What we'd like to do now is highlight the many characteristics that we've observed as the force behind what makes people go far in their careers.

Positively Positive

Over and over, people who go far and get what they want approach life with a "can-do" attitude. Positive thinking is by far the most important resource we've seen people use to get where they want to go. Negative "can't-do" thinking, on the other hand, is a roadblock that has hindered more people than we could even begin to tell. We've said it again and again, you have to think something is possible in order for it to be possible—it's really that simple. Imagining really is the first step toward making it so—whatever "it" is for you. We don't want you to be complex about it—there are too many complexities that bog us down already. Just think positively, don't be abstract, don't doubt, don't try to figure it out. Imagine what you want, believe that it's possible to get, and believe that you are the person who can get it!

Enthusiasm Sells

Take imagination and enthusiasm and hitch the two together. Then fix your gaze on the farthest star and forget the weather.

—Anonymous

A positive attitude is most commonly expressed as enthusiasm—that singularly infectious effervescent way some people have. Equally or even more prevalent than intelligence, credentials, talent, and diligence in getting what you want is an enthusiastic attitude. Enthusiastic people are so upbeat in expressing what they want that they somehow manage—through sheer positive energy—to sell others on their plans! By radiating so much confidence in what they want, no one ever seems to stop to doubt that they will get it—they don't get the chance. Approach anything with a "can-do" invincibility and more often than not, it can be done!—it's like a self-fulfilling prophecy.

Often when people urge us to "just think positive" or "try to be more enthusiastic," we discard the advice thinking that there are positive people and not-so-positive people. If we are not so positive, we doubt that we really can become more positive. We also tend to equate optimism and enthusiasm with being a bit too perky or Pollyanna—somehow they got a bad rap, most likely from some die-hard pessimist. The truth is studies have revealed that optimists do better in school, have better health, earn more money, have happier marriages, are closer to their children, and perhaps even live longer!

We believe positive thinking, optimism, and enthusiasm can be learned. How many opportunities have been squandered by people who talk themselves out of doing something before they even try? Too many! Conversely, how many stories have we heard about people who have had dreams, believed in them, believed in themselves and the abundant possibilities that fill the universe, pursued their dreams and turned them into reality? Plenty!

Where you fall in the spectrum depends on where you place yourself—where you choose to be. Learning how to think positive involves learning how to think about what's possible and not about what's impossible. When you find yourself looking at dead bolts, challenge yourself to find ways to unlock them! Look for the open doors to your plans and take detours around the ones that are closed. When you say you want something, say it as if you mean it! Don't just tell people what you want to do. Convince them that it's possible! Paint the picture—make it vivid—and let them dream your dream with you! It really is how you think, not what you think, that determines whether you go forward or stay still—whether you approach life with or without positivity and enthusiasm.

The All-Important People Factors

Beyond positive thinking, there are other less talked about traits—but tremendously important ones—that take people a long way toward getting what they want. In fact they are so instrumental that we have dubbed them the "people factors." These positive, people-oriented forces include friendliness and kindness, courtesy and consideration, trust and trustworthiness, helpfulness, and having a positive regard and acceptance of others. All of the people factors have to do with how we treat others. No one can deny that they don't enjoy working with or being around nice people. And if you're a nice person who treats others with warmth, respect, and good feeling, you'll go farther than someone who doesn't.

The Good Chemistry of Kindness

Everyone likes nice people. We like being around them at work, we like having them in our families, waiting on us when we go out to dinner, helping us with a problem at our banks, with our cars, on the telephone, and when we ask for directions. Most of us, too, like being nice. The world, in general, is a much more pleasant place when it is filled with friendly and helpful people. Everyone has a "nice person" story, just as everyone has a "not-so-nice" person story. With a special focus on the work arena, we'd like to tell a few of ours.

It's undeniable that nice people are often rewarded in their jobs for their pleasant ways. We met Frank at a talk we gave in Houston several years ago. The president of a large hotel chain, Frank was a laid-back, don't-forget-to-smell-the-flowers, good-morning-ma'am type of Texas gentleman. He did not by any means fit the fast-paced corporate executive mold. His approach to managing the people who managed his company's hotels was simple: treat them as if they were your next-door neighbor.

Everybody who worked for Frank loved him. They'd call him and he'd speak to them directly. He called everyone by his or her first name, never put much importance on titles (never even used his own), and tried to help people out when they came to him with a problem. His informality made him very accessible and likable. People treated him like a friend instead of a superior, which he said was the biggest factor in being able to work with employees instead of around them. "The more personal a company is, the more effective. We're in the business to make people feel comfortable and at home, and there's no better place to start than how you run the business!"

Frank's story is important for two reasons. One—Frank is living proof that nice guys don't always finish last, and two—companies value friendliness and see it as a tremendous asset. Nice people are not only nicer to work with, but they make employees feel good about being at work—which usually increases productivity. Frank, by the way, started in the business as a registration clerk when he was twenty-two!

It's Fair to Care

Hand-in-hand with friendliness and kindness come the rest of the people factors. Courtesy and consideration are important in the workplace and every other place because they stem from caring. Something as simple as letting someone go ahead of you at the Xerox machine has the potential to start someone else's day in a very pleasant way.

Suppose you are at work and you are on your way to a meeting that begins in five minutes. You need a couple of copies of a short report you are going to hand out at the meeting. Someone is at the Xerox machine copying one hundred documents. You wait for them to volunteer to stop what they are doing so you can get your copies made, but they don't. You begin getting anxious and say, "Would you mind if I just get a couple of copies of this report?" They give you an unpleasant and bothered look and you feel even more uncomfortable. Instead of asking again or being rude yourself, you hurry to another department to make your copies. You not only wind up being late, but you feel unnecessarily flustered, anxious, and annoyed—not a great way to start the day!

Now imagine the same scenario, but this time the person Xeroxing sees that you have only a few pages and without even a slight hesitation, offers to stop and let you go ahead—as if they could read your mind. That's exactly what consideration is—being able to know what will make someone feel better and accommodating them without making them ask. Sometimes we're up against our own deadlines and can't always stop what we're doing to accommodate others, but much of the time we can make room for someone else. If it's not something that comes automatically to you, make a conscious effort to be as courteous and considerate as you can. Trying on someone else's point of view is a great way to demonstrate caring and compassion. Like anything else, practice makes perfect!

Trusted Wisdom

Trust is also an important people factor—one that works in many ways. Trusting others and being given a message of trust by others inspire a tremendous amount of confidence as well as loyalty. If someone trusts you to run a company well, you'll probably run it well. If, on the other hand, you sense someone looking over your shoulder at all times—filling you with messages of doubt—your performance will necessarily be negatively affected. Not only does that kind of treatment create the very doubt it puts out, it breeds contempt and resentment—which also have a negative effect on performance. If you are trusted to make a good decision, you'll probably put everything you've got into making the best decision you can. Most people capably shoulder the responsibilities they're given. If you trust the people around you, you can count on the fact that they'll try to fulfill your good expectations of them!

Live and Help Live

The value of helpfulness speaks for itself. Everyone knows what it's like to work with a helpful person, just as everyone knows what it's like to work with someone who's not helpful. We heard a story at a seminar in New York about a woman who was terrified about losing her job when her company introduced computers in her department. She was an accounts manager and had spent fifteen years keeping records the old-fashioned way—on paper in files. She had tremendous anxiety about operating a computer, so much, in fact, that she was about to resign before anyone could discover her dread.

When talking with a friend about her anxiety, her friend reassured her that everyone who has never worked on computers experiences anxiety. Her friend said, "No one is born knowing how to operate a computer anymore than anyone is born knowing how to read—but you learn." What her friend had said struck a very familiar chord with her. When she was young she thought that reading was something only very smart people could learn and was convinced that she never could. When she began learning to read, she was filled with a tremendous sense of power and confidence. Now she thought maybe the same thing could happen with computers.

Feeling reassured, she began thinking what she could do to ease her fear of computers. She remembered a new accounts clerk in her department had once worked as a word processor at a finance company. She approached him with her problem and asked if he could help. Glad to help and flattered to have been asked, he volunteered to come in an hour early each morning to tutor her on the computers her company had already been using in the purchasing department.

After just one week—five hours of coaching—she felt very comfortable with the idea of switching over to computers. The accounts clerk warned her that they will have a different kind of software for accounts, but told her not to worry—that she'd learn that, too. The main thing, he said, was feeling comfortable with what to do with a keyboard. She felt the same kind of power and confidence she had felt when she was six years old! What had seemed a nightmare only a week before was now just a new way of doing part of her job! Without help, she would have made herself sick with worry and self-doubt, dreaded her job, and feared for the future.

Helplessly Lost

We heard a similar story in Atlanta, but the outcome wasn't nearly as positive. A woman started a new job as a writer in the communications department of a large corporation. The company used a computer system totally unlike the one she was used to. And although the new system wasn't really difficult to use, no one helped her learn it. When she asked for help, it consisted of someone coming into her office and performing a function in a lightning flash and leaving. She started writing notes in a notebook, but no one executed the various commands slowly enough for her to write them down. When she asked them to go slowly, they'd give her a bothered look that made her feel uncomfortable.

After about a week and a half of this kind of treatment, she hunted down a computer manual and began trudging through it. It was about as clear as mud and served only to frustrate her further. Because of all the time she spent trying to operate the computer, she was late on her first writing project and was beginning to feel totally overwhelmed. She was a good writer but found herself hating her job, doubting her competence, and at a complete loss as to where to turn. She solved the problem by calling in one morning to tell her boss that she had accepted another job!

Lend a Hand

Take time to help others. Remember that people are the building blocks to your own success.

—Anonymous

If there's a way you can help a coworker, help them! Not only is it the right thing to do, it makes everyone's job easier and more pleasant. By being helpful you stand out as a contributor who cares for others as well as the efficiency of your company. Add to that feelings of kindness, consideration, and trust and you become a vital part in creating an ideal work environment. Such a contributor rarely, if ever, goes unrewarded!

Above All: Respect and Dignity

Although all these people factors are important get-ahead traits, we think the most important one is to hold others in high esteem. Having respect and high regard for others is the best way to work as well as the best way to be a human being. So much pain and ill feeling comes with disrespect. In fact all forms of prejudice can be traced to wrongly disrespecting others. Whether the source of difference between or among people is in rank or title, sex, race, religious belief, or socioeconomic status, difference should always be treated with respect and dignity. Instead of thinking in terms of difference, we should think of diversity and welcome the richness it affords.

The Intelligence Quotients

Besides positive thinking and people orientation, Intelligence is the most important in determining how far you go in your profession and in life. The get-ahead traits that belong to intelligence are logic, creativity, and common sense—all the characteristics that concern how you think. We all know that it takes some smarts to do just about anything well, but how you use them is what distinguishes players.

Intelligence, simply, is your capacity to understand things rationally. It is the basis of how you come to know anything. Specific to our purposes here, it is the foundation to how well you learn and master your job, how you solve problems, make decisions, and use common sense. Intelligence, then, is the cognitive wellspring you draw from to do your job well.

Thinking Styles

Besides needing intelligence to gain knowledge to increase our expertise at what we do, we need it to solve problems and make decisions. How we arrive at solutions to problems and decisions, however, depends on how we think—our cognitive style. Research in cognitive psychology has pinpointed two types of thinking—convergent and divergent.

Convergent thinking involves tunneling in on one solution to a problem, and divergent thinking is seeing many solutions. Convergent thinking is most often equated with one's ability to use logic—thinking that goes forward, step-by-step, to arrive at one answer. Divergent thinking is what is most commonly thought of as creativity—thinking that branches out to find many possible answers. Whether you think convergently or divergently, the valued result on the job is your ability to come up with effective solutions and make decisions on your own.

At a conference in San Francisco, a man asked us if we could give some advice concerning a "little problem" he was having at work. He said that he had been turned down four times for a promotion from junior financial analyst to financial analyst. We asked what he thought the reason might be, and he said, "I don't know, my numbers are good, my target stocks are right on the money, my performance reviews are always good, and I always confer with other analysts on any decisions I make." We were suspicious about the last element in his answer and asked, "Do you ever make any decisions on your own?" He replied with a quick "Never!" We asked, "Why not?" A bit stupefied—as if a light went on for the first time—he said, "I don't know, I guess I just wanted to show how conscientious I am."

While the analyst was trying to make points for conscientiousness, he was losing points for not taking the ball in his own hands and making his own decisions. Why would his company make him a full-fledged analyst when a big part of an analyst's job is making decisions about his or her findings? Such a promotion would be risky, at best. Other analysts have their own decisions to make—they certainly don't want to be bogged down with making decisions for other analysts!

Common Sense Is Not Always So Common

The most valued intelligence trait in all walks of life, especially on the job, is common sense. Common sense is intelligence that is mixed with the wisdom of past experience. Simply, it is the ability to make decisions based on what you know is true. Whereas logic and creativity depend on knowledge and inspiration, common sense relies on practical experience—what you know from experience to be true. Amazingly, not everyone applies their past experiences to present situations.

A very bright lawyer friend of ours, who is more than well versed in making logical decisions, is at a loss when it comes to common sense. A person who can quote chapter and verse of every important judicial ruling of the twentieth century can't seem to wrap his mind around the notion that judges get annoyed when you show up late for court! Having been verbally reprimanded more than a dozen times for being late, he still can't seem to allow enough time to change his habit of tardiness. It doesn't take much common sense to realize that annoying a judge is not the best way to represent a client who is totally dependent on that judge's mercy!

Ingenuity Goes a Long Way

It's better to light a candle than curse the darkness.
—*Eleanor Roosevelt*

Insightfulness and ingenuity are critical intelligence traits and are often the ones that determine whether you stand out or blend in with the woodwork. Insight is the ability to see and understand the inner nature of things, while ingenuity has to do with how clever and original you are. Understanding the "inner nature" of things means knowing what plan will work in a given situation and what plan won't work; ingenuity means you can come up with a way to put the right plan into motion.

Ninety-nine Percent Perspiration

Nothing in the world can take the place of persistence.
—*Calvin Coolidge*

We touched a great deal on the "perspiration traits" when we talked about goal getting. Perseverance, diligence, and dedication are paramount to getting what you want and where you want to go. And everything pales beside hard work when it comes to being held in high esteem by an employer. After all, what common bottom line do all employers share? Production! When push comes to shove, diligent workers are usually the most valued resource in every work place.

A woman who attended a talk we gave in Minneapolis said that she felt she was being overlooked for her clever contributions at work. A middle management executive in customer services for a major airlines, she regularly came up with new ways to handle customer complaints. Among her innovations were a training program for customer service clerks to address complaints in a highly personal and responsive way, a system of following up complaints by phone and by personalized letters, and an incentive program that rewarded clerks with the best records in satisfying dissatisfied customers. Her grievance was that she had not been moved up to top management by now.

After some probing, she confessed that she didn't devote enough time to some of her other job requirements because of the time she spent coming up with innovations—thinking that they would be her ticket to recognition. "Chances are," we suggested, "your bosses are paying attention to the things you're not paying attention to! If you're not performing everything expected of you in your current position, your company probably doesn't trust you to handle all the new tasks in a new position."

Professional Personality Profile

We've looked at all the traits people we've encountered have told us have helped them get ahead in their work. We want you to take a minute now to look in your work mirror and list the qualities you see. What is it about you that makes you do your job well and stand out as a crucial player? What is it about you that holds you back from being all you can be or getting all you want from your job? We have come up with some questions to assist you in taking a closer look at your professional personality profile. Please jot down your answers—and any other thoughts that occur to you—on a separate piece of paper.

- Do you have a positive attitude about your work?
- Do you believe that you can advance in your career?
- Do you approach your job with enthusiasm?
- Do you carry around a negative feeling about what you do?
- Do you complain about your job demands?
- Are you friendly with coworkers, bosses, and clients?
- Do you go out of your way to be helpful at work?
- Do you treat others courteously and with fairness?
- Do you respect other people's opinions?
- Do you trust your bosses and coworkers?
- Do you solve problems and make decisions easily?
- Do you rely on past experience when finding solutions?
- Do you perceive the invisible dynamics of your job?
- Are you innovative about the way you do things?
- Are you open to more than one way of doing things?
- Do you tend to see one answer to problems or many?
- Do you give up on a task easily?
- Do you watch the clock while you're working?
- Do you stay with something until you get it right?

Take a minute to reflect on your answers. Look at your answers and label them as to what traits they involve. If you feel as if there is an area you can improve on, jot down ways you could try. If you care to, map out a strategy to approach a day's work that implements all the positive traits we've talked about. Also jot down an ideal professional profile—a picture of the you you'd most like to be and the traits that go into that you.

Chapter Eleven

A Postscript: Putting Things into Perspective

Before we end our journey with you, some reality checks are in order. We have spent a good deal of time cheering you on to do the things that are most important to you. Before you delve into the rest of your life, take a deep look at how your plans really do fit into your life and what trade-offs might be involved.

Do a Cost-Benefit Analysis on Your Dreams

Companies often perform a cost-benefit analysis before making a major investment or change to make sure the perceived benefits will justify the cost. If the analysis indicates the cost is warranted by the benefits to be received, the company makes the investment. Whether a corporation decides to create a new department, open a plant overseas, or invest in new computer software to track inventory, a cost-benefit analysis is essential. We suggest you do the same kind of analysis on your goals and dreams.

Coast to Coast

If you live in New York City and your goal is move to northern California, list the costs and benefits you anticipate in relocating. The benefit column, for example, might include: living in a beautiful place, being near other family members and friends who have made the move, lower cost of living, ideal climate, better roads and highways, lower car insurance rates, better parking, less traffic, lower crime, a feeling of adventure and flexibility, a better place to raise a family, cleaner air, less noise, fewer crowds, and a generally increased quality of life.

The cost column might include: being unemployed, depleting savings while unemployed, the stress of looking for a new job, adapting to unfamiliar surroundings, leaving friends and family in New York, loss of professional contacts on the East Coast, moving expenses, traveling expenses, giving up the rich culture of big city life, and the general upheaval of change.

Making a decision in this scenario is pretty tough. California obviously has more going for it than New York, but giving up a job certainly deserves more weight than better highways and roads. According to this analysis, relocating seems to offer more long-range benefits, but staying put has more short-range ones.

The next step is to weigh the main cost against the main benefit. In this case you have to weigh giving up an income against enjoying where you live. When it comes down to the nitty-gritty, our choice would be to move to California, since one of the reasons we work hard at our jobs is to have the means to lead a life we enjoy. If you don't like where you live, why are you paying a good part of your salary to live there? Chances are you will find a good job in California! In time you will be reaping only benefits.

Taking a Pass

It is common to go through a lot of trial and error when it comes to deciding whether your plans involve trade-offs that are too costly. A couple we once worked with had a dream of buying a fast-food franchise and working for themselves for the rest of their work lives. After a lot of research and evaluating, they honed in on a McDonald's franchise in Denver. Purchasing the franchise translated into a lot of their dreams coming true—owning their own business, being their own bosses, working in the food and beverage industry, and living in the mountains.

After talking with several other McDonald's franchise owners, however, who all told stories of working around the clock for the first four years while the business got on its feet, they were a bit dismayed. At ages forty-seven and forty-four, they didn't feel as if they really wanted to put that much time into getting a business off the ground. It wasn't the hard work as much as it was the idea of giving up their two vacations a year, which they loved more than anything. Also, they had just filled the last twenty-plus years of their lives with hard work! They concluded, "One year of paying dues is one thing, two years is another, but four?—no way!" Deciding that the trade-offs were too steep, they opted not to buy the franchise.

Testing the Waters

A couple we met at a seminar in New York, and eventually became friends with, had their hearts set on living in London for a few years. We suggested that they test-market their move by taking an extended vacation there before they uprooted their lives. In the three weeks they were there, it rained two and a half weeks straight! And they both hated inclement weather!

While there, too, they found the cost of living and real estate extremely high, and that the English didn't have much taste for successful, outspoken women entrepreneurs—which was exactly what one of our friends was! Needless to say, the reality of London didn't quite measure up to their dream.

Whether you do a cost-benefit analysis, measure risks against rewards, test-market your plans, or do as a bookkeeper does and subtract debits from credits, the important thing is that you are sure of the trade-offs involved in pursuing your dreams. Sometimes, however, dreams resist any form of rational analysis, and the only way of knowing their outcome is to pursue them. These dreams are usually always dreams of the heart.

Dreams of the Heart

A twenty-eight-year-old newspaper editor we met in New York told us the story of her dream. After coming to New York on vacation, she met the person of her dreams. She lived and worked in Oakland, California, and spent the next four months having a long-distance love affair. There were plenty of long weekends back and forth in both directions, and more money than we care to think of spent on telephone bills.

Unable to relocate because he owned his own business, her boyfriend was stuck in New York City and the ball was in her court. The cost-benefit of moving to New York was totally skewed against relocating—giving up a great job at a big newspaper with a tremendous opportunity for advancement, leaving family, lifelong friends, a state she loved, a beautiful apartment with a view of San Francisco, a sports car, and a tutoring business she had built up since her college days. The benefit was singular—being with the person she loved. And although everyone she knew advised her against going, she followed her heart to New York City. Six years later she is happy with her choice, despite never having regained the same financial security or job satisfaction that she enjoyed in California. The sacrifices, however, were worth what she considers to be a much larger happiness and security.

A Last Word from Us to You

We have come to the end of our journey with one hope—that your journey is just beginning. As you venture out on your quest to find, keep, and nurture what is dearest to you in your infinitely abundant life, we wish you luck, courage, and confidence. If you should ever need us, we offer you our permanent friendship in the preceding pages. Before we say good-bye, we'd like to leave you with some parting thoughts that we hope will help you along your way.

We are all looking for ideal worlds within one very real one. The impulse to be better, to have better lives, is very strong in us. Besides being a very strong cultural message, it's a biological one as well. Those great frontal lobes—where abstract thought is born—is the place ideals are manufactured. The ideal of having a better life is a pure abstraction—something we can imagine and generate desire for. But in the very real world that encircles our ideals, we must forewarn ourselves that we can't always get what we want. And even if we do, something else in our lives, perhaps even things very dear to us, must give.

If we are going back to school at night, working long hours, studying a pursuit, we necessarily must give less time to other things, such as time with our children or friends—that's the real world. The first law of energy is that there is no such thing as a free lunch. The energy we spend on one endeavor limits how much we can spend on another.

What a terrible thing to work very hard at something and feel that because we have, something else in our lives is missing. What a terrible thing to work hard at making a dream come true and finding out it's not all we made it out to be in our imaginative longing. We must remind ourselves that the process of making our lives better is never perfect and is always ongoing.

Perfection, in fact, probably never can exist because it is beyond the human ken. Being human is to be driven to be better. Our love of challenge is in the chemistry of who we are. When one challenge is met, we soon crave another. We are insatiable. If all our challenges were ever to be met, in fact, we would probably feel dissatisfied. We thrive on our discontent. It is our very motivation to be content.

Our ongoing movement toward contentment not only defines us, it also fills our time, nurtures our wisdom, and keeps us open to the myriad sources of fulfillment that surround us. While seeking contentment, we find things that surprise us along the way. If we gave up our search after one pursuit, we'd miss out on potential wellsprings to our happiness. Keep this always close at heart, in mind, because there will always be some new thing that we want, want to change, want to be different. Expect it. It's very much a part—if not the heart—of who we are.

Sometimes an even bigger challenge than fulfilling our ideals is to open up to the beauty—the joys—in our real worlds. The greatest perfection is perfection with rough edges since that's how we and the world are put together. Appreciating our frailties, the ordinary, simple joys in our real lives, and the never-quite-finished quality about who we are is probably the most creative leap we can ever make and the most beautiful dream we can ever dream.

Suggested Reading

Bateson, Mary Catherine. *Composing a Life*. New York: Penguin, 1990.

Bethel, Sheila Murray. *Making a Difference: 12 Qualities That Make You a Leader*. New York: Berkley Publishing Group, 1990.

Bisbee, Bob. *Steer Your Own Career*. New York: Nichols Publishing, 1988.

Briles, Judith. *The Confidence Factor*. New York: MasterMedia, 1990.

Brown, Jackson H., Jr. *Life's Little Instruction Book*. Nashville: Rutledge Hill Press, 1992.

Brown, Les. *Live Your Dreams*. New York: William Morrow and Company, 1992.

Burton, M. L., and R. A. Wedemeyer. *In Transition*. New York: HarperCollins, 1991.

Covey, Stephen R. *The 7 Habits of Highly Effective People*. New York: Simon & Schuster, 1989.

Dinkmeyer, D., Ph.D., and L. Losoncy, Ph.D. *The Encouragement Book*. New York: Prentice-Hall, 1980.

Fulghum, Robert. *All I Really Need to Know I Learned in Kindergarten*. New York: Villard Books, 1990.

Gawain, Shakti. *Creative Visualization*. New York: Bantam Books, 1978.

Goman, Carol Kinsey, Ph.D. *The Loyalty Factor: Building Trust in Today's Workplace*. New York: MasterMedia, 1991.

Hedrick, Lucy H. *365 Ways to Save Time*. New York: William Morrow and Company, 1992.

Heller, Robert. *Super Self: The Art and Science of Self-Management.* New York: Atheneum, 1979.

Jampolsky, Gerald G., M.D. *One Person Can Make a Difference.* New York: Bantam Doubleday Dell, 1990.

Johnson, Spencer. *"Yes" or "No": The Guide to Better Decisions.* New York: HarperCollins, 1992.

Kanchier, Carole, Ph.D. *Dare to Change Your Job—And Your Life.* New York: MasterMedia, 1991.

Kirsh, M. M. *How to Get Off the Fast Track and Live a Life Money Can't Buy.* New York: HarperCollins, 1991.

Leeds, Dorothy. *Marketing Yourself.* New York: HarperCollins, 1991.

Ludeman, Kate, Ph.D. *The Worth Ethic.* New York: E. P. Dutton, 1989.

Mandino, Og. *The Greatest Salesman in the World.* New York: Bantam Books, 1968.

May, Rollo. *The Courage to Create.* New York: Bantam Books, 1975.

————. *The Discovery of Being.* New York: W. W. Norton and Company, 1983.

McGinnes, Alan Loy. *The Power of Optimism.* New York: Harper & Row, 1990.

Morrisey, George, L. *Creating Your Future.* San Francisco: Barrett-Koehler Publishers, 1992.

Nierenberg, Gerald. *The Art of Creative Thinking.* New York: Simon & Schuster, 1982.

Peale, Norman Vincent. *The Power of Positive Thinking.* New York: Fawcett Crest, 1963.

————. *The Power of the Plus Factor.* New Jersey: Fleming H. Revell Co., 1987.

————. *The Power of Positive Living.* New York: Bantam Doubleday Dell, 1990.

Robbins, Anthony. *Awaken the Giant Within.* New York: Summit Books, 1991.

Roddick, Anita. *Body and Soul.* New York: Crown Publishers, 1991.

Swain, Madeleine, and Robert Swain. *Out the Organization: New Career Opportunities for the 1990's.* New York: MasterMedia, 1992.

Waitley, Denis. *Timing Is Everything.* Nashville: Thomas Nelson Publishers, 1992.

Williams, A. L. *All You Can Do Is All You Can Do.* Nashville: Thomas Nelson Publishers, 1988.

Winston, Stephanie. *The Organized Executive.* New York: Time Warner Books, 1983.

Ziglar, Zig. *Top Performance.* New York: Berkley Publishing Group, 1986.

Index

accomplishment, sense of, 33–34
acting, 7–8
alliances, 81–82, 121
attitude, 97
avocations, 85

bosses, as obstacle to
    self-promotion, 132
Bowe, Riddick, 71
Briles, Judith, 22, 23

chambers of commerce, 82–83
changing jobs, 108
City Slickers, 41
Clinton, Bill, 32
college placement offices, 82
Columbus, Christopher, 102
commitment, 52–54
common sense, 145–46
communications, 122
    clarity in, 124
    in self-promotion, 125
    see also networking
company newsletters, 83
complaints, 95
computers, fears of, 141–42
confidence, see self-confidence
conformity, 11
contacts, 80
    see also networking

convergent thinking, 144
Coolidge, Calvin, 146
cost-benefit analyses, 149
    of relocating, 150, 152–53
courtesy and consideration,
    139–40
crises, confidence and, 22
Crystal, Billy, 41

debt, 85–86
dignity, 143
direction, sense of, 50–52
discipline, 52
Disney, Walt, 38
distractions, 72
divergent thinking, 144
drama, 7–8
drive, 49–50

Edison, Thomas, 37–38
education, 84–85
Einstein, Albert, 38
Emerson, Ralph Waldo, 31
employee-involvement programs,
    114–15
employment, 107–8
    employee-involvement programs
    in, 114–15
    getting the most out of, 112–13
    getting through contacts, 81–82

159

employment (*continued*)
  "greener pastures" elsewhere, 113–14
  hidden agendas in, 99–100
  knowing your business in, 126
  making more pleasant, 111–12
  networking in, 121–24
  public sources of, 82–83
  risks in, 100–101
  rule-breaking in, 97–99
  satisfaction in, 105–6, 108–11, 116–19
  search for meaning in, 115
  self-definition through, 18–19
  self-identity beyond, 115–16
  self-promotion in, 125–26
  success at, 43
  suggestions at, 95
enthusiasm, 136–37
experience, 84

failure
  fear of, 8–9
  learning from, 37–38
fears
  of computers, 141–42
  of failing, 8–9
flexibility, 54–56
forgiveness of loans, 86
Freud, Sigmund, 106
Frost, Robert, 64

gender, self-promotion and, 132–33
goals, 24, 58–59
  changing, 60–61
  commitment and perseverance in, 52–54
  direction and purpose in, 50–52

distractions and, 72
  drive and motivation in, 49–50
  flexibility in, 54–56
  mapping strategies for, 66–67
  persistence in, 56–57
  realistic expectations in, 57–58
  self-discipline and, 52
  setting, 47
  strategies to reach, 59, 63–64, 65–66
  timetables for reaching, 59–60
  see also strategies
Gorman, Carol Kinsey, 114
"greener pastures," 113–14

helpfulness, 141–42, 143
hidden agendas, 99–100
Holmes, Oliver Wendell, 3
Holyfield, Evander, 71
Housman, A.E., 47
human resources, 79–81
  alliances and, 81–82

ingenuity, 146
innovation, 97–98, 102–3
intelligence, 144
  common sense and, 145–46
  ingenuity and, 146
  thinking styles and, 144–45
It's a Wonderful Life, 28

jobs, *see* employment
job satisfaction, 105–6, 108–11, 116–19
  "greener pastures" and, 113–14
  improving, 111–12
  search for meaning and, 115
job security, 43

kindness, 138–39

Lincoln, Abraham, 102
loans, 86
loans, debts from, 85–86
Lombardi, Vincent, 93
Longfellow, Henry Wadsworth, 65

Madonna, 125
Mansfield, Katherine, 63
men, self-promotion by, 133
monetary security, 33, 44
    myth of, 34–37
Morley, Christopher, 31
Moses, Grandma, 6
motivation, 49–50, 59
myths
    of confidence, 21–22
    of money, 34–37

negative experiences, 23–24
negative thinking, 135
    on self-promotion, 131–32
networking, 121–22
    alliances in, 81–82
    asking for things and, 122–23
    clarity in, 124
    contacts and, 80
    focusing in, 123
    identifying key players in,
        126–27
    knowing your business in, 126
    self-promotion in, 125–26
Nietzsche, Friedrich, 22

optimism, 136–37

parents
    approval by, 16–17
    disapproval by, 17–18
patents, 86
Peale, Norman Vincent, 15, 20
people factors, 137–38
    courtesy and consideration as,
        139–40
    helpfulness as, 141–42, 143
    kindness as, 138–39
    respect and dignity as, 143
    trust as, 140
perfectionism, 38
perseverance, 52–54
persistence, 56–57, 72
personal presentation, 129–30
personal resources, 86–88
placement offices, 82
plans, see strategies
positive thinking, 23, 88, 135–36
    enthusiasm and, 136–37
practical resources, 84–85
prejudices, 143
professional personality profiles,
        147–48
public resources, 82–83
published resources, 83
punishments, 67–69

quality-of-life, 39
    "secret of," 39–40

relocating
    cost-benefit analyses of, 150,
        152–53
    public resources for information
        on, 82–83
resources, 88–91

resources (*continued*)
  alliances as, 81–82
  particular, 85–86
  people as, 79–81
  personal, 86–88
  practical, 84–85
  public, 82–83
  published, 83
respect, 143
rewards, 67–69
risk, 24–26, 100–101
  inhibition toward, 101–2
Robinson, Edwin Arlington, 34–35
role models, 80–81
Roosevelt, Eleanor, 146
Rousseau, Jean-Jacques, 84
rule-breaking, 97–99

satisfaction, job, 105–6, 108–11,
    116–19
  "greener pastures" and, 113–14
  improving, 111–12
  search for meaning and, 115
Schopenauer, Arthur, 125
security
  job security, 43
  monetary, 33–37, 44
self-confidence, 19
  belief in self in, 26–27
  crisis and, 22
  lack of, 20–21
  myth of, 21–22
  positive thinking in, 23
  risk taking and, 24–26
self-definition, employment in,
    18–19
self-discipline, 52
self-doubt, 102

self-promotion, 125–26, 134
  assessment of, 130–31
  creating spotlights in, 128–29
  gender differences in, 132–33
  getting started in, 133
  negative thinking on, 131–32
  performance and, 127–28
  personal presentation in, 129–30
self-worth
  parental approval in, 16–17
  parental disapproval in, 17–18
sense of accomplishment, 33–34
Shakespeare, William, 1
Stein, Gertrude, 7
Steinbeck, John, 105
Stevens, Wallace, 103
Stewart, Jimmy, 28
strategies, for reaching goals,
    59–60, 63–64, 65–66, 69–70,
    76–77
  mapping, 66–67
  mental walk-throughs in, 71–73
  minor adjustments in, 73–74
  rewards and punishments in,
    67–69
  testing, 74–75
student loans, 86
success, 43–45
  employment and, 43
  enthusiasm in, 136–37
  inner-focus in, 38–39
  kindness and, 138–39
  learning from failures and, 37–38
  money and, 34–37
  new measurements of, 32–33
  people factors in, 137–38
  perfectionism and, 38
  positive thinking in, 135–36

success (*continued*)
   putting into the future, 41
   quality-of-life in, 39
   self as agent of, 42–43
   self-confidence and, 21–22
   sense of accomplishment in,
      33–34
suggestions, at work, 95
Swain, Madeleine, 123
Swain, Robert, 123

theater, 7–8
thinking styles, 144–45
Thoreau, Henry David, 31
timetables for reaching goals, 59–60

Toklas, Alice B., 7
travel, 4–6
Trump, Donald, 125
trust, 140

vacations, 5–6, 111–12
volunteer work, 49

Wilde, Oscar, 79
Williams, William Carlos, 70
W.L. Gore & Associates, 114
women, self-promotion by, 132–33
work, *see* employment

Ziglar, Zig, 31–32

About the Authors

Jeri Sedlar is the president of her own communications company as well as editor-at-large of *Working Woman* magazine and a recognized authority on women and career-related issues. Through her work with large and small companies, associations, and government agencies, Sedlar has motivated thousands of women to get off the bleachers and onto the playing field.

Rick Miners is the president of Goodrich and Sherwood Company, a human resources consulting firm, and has held marketing and sales positions at several major corporations. He has written and lectured extensively on career issues and is frequently interviewed on television and radio.

Both authors currently live in New York City.

Additional copies of *On Target* may be ordered by sending a check for $11.95 (please add the following for postage and handling: $2.00 for the first copy, $1.00 for each added copy) to:

MasterMedia Limited
17 East 89th Street
New York, NY 10128
(212) 260-5600
(800) 334-8232
(212) 546-7638 (fax)

The authors are available for speeches. Please contact MasterMedia's Speakers' Bureau for availability and fee arrangements. Call Tony Colao at 908-359-1612; fax: 908-359-1647.

Other MasterMedia Books

To order MasterMedia books, either visit your local bookstore or call (800)334-8232.

THE PREGNANCY AND MOTHERHOOD DIARY: Planning the First Year of Your Second Career, by Susan Schiffer Stautberg, is the first and only undated appointment diary that shows how to manage pregnancy and career. ($12.95 spiral-bound)

CITIES OF OPPORTUNITY: Finding the Best Place to Work, Live and Prosper in the 1990's and Beyond, by Dr. John Tepper Marlin, explores the job and living options for the next decade and into the next century. This consumer guide and handbook, written by one of the world's experts on cities, selects and features forty-six American cities and metropolitan areas. ($13.95 paper, $24.95 cloth)

THE DOLLARS AND SENSE OF DIVORCE, by Dr. Judith Briles, is the first book to combine practical tips on overcoming the legal hurdles by planning finances before, during, and after divorce. ($10.95 paper)

OUT THE ORGANIZATION: New Career Opportunities for the 1990s, by Robert and Madeleine Swain, is written for the millions of Americans whose jobs are no longer safe, whose companies are not loyal, and who face futures of uncertainty. It gives advice on finding a new job or starting your own business. ($12.95 paper)

AGING PARENTS AND YOU: A Complete Handbook to Help You Help Your Elders Maintain a Healthy, Productive and Independent Life, by Eugenia Anderson-Ellis, is a complete guide to providing care to aging relatives. It gives practical advice and resources to the adults who are helping their elders lead productive and independent lives. Revised and updated. ($9.95 paper)

CRITICISM IN YOUR LIFE: How to Give It, How to Take It, How to Make It Work for You, by Dr. Deborah Bright, offers practical advice, in an upbeat, readable, and realistic fashion, for turning criticism into control. Charts and diagrams guide the reader into managing criticism from bosses, spouses, children, friends, neighbors, in-laws, and business relations. ($17.95 cloth)

BEYOND SUCCESS: How Volunteer Service Can Help You Begin Making a Life Instead of Just a Living, by John F. Raynolds III and Eleanor Raynolds, C.B.E., is a unique how-to book targeted at business and professional people considering volunteer work, senior citizens who wish to fill leisure time meaningfully, and students trying out various career options. The book is filled with interviews with celebrities, CEOs, and average citizens who talk about the benefits of service work. ($19.95 cloth)

MANAGING IT ALL: Time-Saving Ideas for Career, Family, Relationships, and Self, by Beverly Benz Treuille and Susan Schiffer Stautberg, is written for women who are juggling careers and families. Over two hundred career women (ranging from a TV anchorwoman to an investment banker) were interviewed. The book contains many humorous anecdotes on saving time and improving the quality of life for self and family. ($9.95 paper)

YOUR HEALTHY BODY, YOUR HEALTHY LIFE: How to Take Control of Your Medical Destiny, by Donald B. Louria, M.D., provides precise advice and strategies that will help you to live a long and healthy life. Learn also about nutrition, exercise, vitamins, and medication, as well as how to control risk factors for major diseases. Revised and updated. ($12.95 paper)

THE CONFIDENCE FACTOR: How Self-Esteem Can Change Your Life, by Dr. Judith Briles, is based on a nationwide survey of six thousand men and women. Briles explores why women so often feel a lack of self-confidence and have a poor opinion of themselves. She offers step-by-step advice on becoming the person you want to be. ($9.95 paper, $18.95 cloth)

THE SOLUTION TO POLLUTION: 101 Things You Can Do to Clean Up Your Environment, by Laurence Sombke, offers step-by-step techniques on how to conserve more energy, start a recycling center, choose biodegradable products, and even proceed with individual environmental cleanup projects. ($7.95 paper)

TAKING CONTROL OF YOUR LIFE: The Secrets of Successful Enterprising Women, by Gail Blanke and Kathleen Walas, is based on the authors' professional experience with Avon Products' Women of Enterprise Awards, given each year to outstanding women entrepreneurs. The authors offer a specific plan to help you gain control over your life, and include business tips and quizzes as well as beauty and lifestyle information. ($17.95 cloth)

SIDE-BY-SIDE STRATEGIES: How Two-Career Couples Can Thrive in the Nineties, by Jane Hershey Cuozzo and S. Diane Graham, describes how two-career couples can learn the difference between competing with a spouse and becoming a supportive power partner. Published in hardcover as *Power Partners.* ($10.95 paper, $19.95 cloth)

DARE TO CONFRONT! How to Intervene When Someone You Care About Has an Alcohol or Drug Problem, by Bob Wright and Deborah George Wright, shows the reader how to use the step-by-step methods of professional interventionists to motivate drug-dependent people to accept the help they need. ($17.95 cloth)

WORK WITH ME! How to Make the Most of Office Support Staff, by Betsy Lazary, shows you how to find, train, and nurture the "perfect" assistant and how to best utilize your support staff professionals. ($9.95 paper)

MANN FOR ALL SEASONS: Wit and Wisdom from The Washington Post's *Judy Mann,* by Judy Mann, shows the columnist at her best as she writes about women, families, and the impact and politics of the women's revolution. ($9.95 paper, $19.95 cloth)

THE SOLUTION TO POLLUTION IN THE WORKPLACE, by Laurence Sombke, Terry M. Robertson and Elliot M. Kaplan, supplies employees with everything they need to know about cleaning up their workspace, including recycling, using energy efficiently, conserving water and buying recycled products and nontoxic supplies. ($9.95 paper)

THE ENVIRONMENTAL GARDENER: The Solution to Pollution for Lawns and Gardens, by Laurence Sombke, focuses on what each of us can do to protect our endangered plant life. A practical source-book and shopping guide. ($8.95 paper)

THE LOYALTY FACTOR: Building Trust in Today's Workplace, by Carol Kinsey Goman, Ph.D., offers techniques for restoring commitment and loyalty in the workplace. ($9.95 paper)

DARE TO CHANGE YOUR JOB—AND YOUR LIFE, by Carole Kanchier, Ph.D., provides a look at career growth and development throughout the life cycle. ($9.95 paper)

MISS AMERICA: In Pursuit of the Crown, by Ann-Marie Bivans, is an authorized guidebook to the Pageant, containing eyewitness accounts, complete historical data, and a realistic look at the trials and triumphs of the potential Miss Americas. ($19.95 paper, $27.50 cloth; b & w and color photos)

POSITIVELY OUTRAGEOUS SERVICE: New and Easy Ways to Win Customers for Life, by T. Scott Gross, identifies what the consumers of the nineties really want and how businesses can develop effective marketing strategies to answer those needs. ($14.95 paper)

BREATHING SPACE: Living and Working at a Comfortable Pace in a Sped-Up Society, by Jeff Davidson, helps readers to handle information and activity overload, and gain greater control over their lives. ($10.95 paper)

TWENTYSOMETHING: Managing and Motivating Today's New Work Force, by Lawrence J. Bradford, Ph.D., and Claire Raines, M.A., examines the work orientation of the younger generation, offering managers in businesses of all kinds a practical guide to better understand and supervise their young employees. ($22.95 cloth)

REAL LIFE 101: The Graduate's Guide to Survival, by Susan Kleinman, supplies welcome advice to those facing "real life" for the first time, focusing on work, money, health, and how to deal with freedom and responsibility. ($9.95 paper)

BALANCING ACTS! Juggling Love, Work, Family, and Recreation, by Susan Schiffer Stautberg and Marcia L. Worthing, provides strategies to achieve a balanced life by reordering priorities and setting realistic goals. ($12.95 paper)

REAL BEAUTY . . . REAL WOMEN: A Handbook for Making the Best of Your Own Good Looks, by Kathleen Walas, International Beauty and Fashion Director of Avon Products, offers expert advice on beauty and fashion to women of all ages and ethnic backgrounds. ($19.50 paper; in full color)

THE LIVING HEART BRAND NAME SHOPPER'S GUIDE (Revised and Updated), by Michael E. DeBakey, M.D., Antonio M. Gotto, Jr., M.D., D.Phil., Lynne W. Scott, M.A., R.D./L.D., and John P. Foreyt, Ph.D., lists brand-name supermarket products that are low in fat, saturated fatty acids, and cholesterol. ($14.95 paper)

MANAGING YOUR CHILD'S DIABETES, by Robert Wood Johnson IV, Sale Johnson, Casey Johnson, and Susan Kleinman, brings help to families trying to understand diabetes and control its effects. ($10.95 paper)

STEP FORWARD: Sexual Harassment in the Workplace, What You Need to Know, by Susan L. Webb, presents the facts for dealing with sexual harassment on the job. ($9.95 paper)

A TEEN'S GUIDE TO BUSINESS: The Secrets to a Successful Enterprise, by Linda Menzies, Oren S. Jenkins, and Rickell R. Fisher, provides solid information about starting your own business or working for one. ($7.95 paper)

GLORIOUS ROOTS: Recipes for Healthy, Tasty Vegetables, by Laurence Sombke, celebrates the taste, texture, and versatility of root vegetables. Contains recipes for appetizers, soups, stews, and baked, broiled, and stir-fried dishes—even desserts. ($12.95 paper)

THE OUTDOOR WOMAN: A Handbook to Adventure, by Patricia Hubbard and Stan Wass, details the lives of adventurous outdoor women and offers their ideas on how you can incorporate exciting outdoor experiences into your life. ($14.95 paper; with photos)

FLIGHT PLAN FOR LIVING: The Art of Self-Encouragement, by Patrick O'Dooley, is a life guide organized like a pilot's flight checklist, which ensures you'll be flying "clear on top" throughout your life. ($17.95 cloth)

HOW TO GET WHAT YOU WANT FROM ALMOST ANYBODY, by T. Scott Gross, shows how to get great service, negotiate better prices, and always get what you pay for. ($9.95 paper)

TEAMBUILT: Making Teamwork Work, by Mark Sanborn, teaches business how to improve productivity, without increasing resources or expenses, by building teamwork among employers. ($19.95 cloth)

THE BIG APPLE BUSINESS AND PLEASURE GUIDE: 501 Ways to Work Smarter, Play Harder, and Live Better in New York City, by Muriel Siebert and Susan Kleinman, offers visitors and New Yorkers alike advice on how to do business in the city as well as how to enjoy its attractions. ($9.95 paper)

FINANCIAL SAVVY FOR WOMEN: A Money Book for Women of All Ages, by Dr. Judith Briles, divides a woman's monetary lifespan into six phases, discusses the specific areas to be addressed at each stage, and demonstrates how to create a sound lifelong money game plan. ($14.95 paper)

MIND YOUR OWN BUSINESS: And Keep It in the Family, by Marcy Syms, COO of Syms Corporation, is an effective guide for any organization, small or large, facing what is documented to be the toughest step in managing a family business—making the transition to the new generation. ($18.95 cloth)

KIDS WHO MAKE A DIFFERENCE, by Joyce M. Roché and Marie Rodriguez, with Phyllis Schneider, is a surprising and inspiring document of some of today's toughest challenges being met—by teenagers and kids! Their courage and creativity allowed them to find practical solutions. ($8.95 paper; with photos)

ROSEY GRIER'S ALL-AMERICAN HEROS: Multicultural Success Stories, by Roosevelt "Rosey" Grier, is a wonderful collection of personal histories, told in their own words by prominent African-Americans, Latins, Asians, and native Americans; each tells of the people in their lives and choices they made in achieving public acclaim and personal success. ($9.95 paper; with portrait photos)

OFFICE BIOLOGY: Why Tuesday Is the Most Productive Day and Other Relevant Facts for Survival in the Workplace, by Edith Weiner and Arnold Brown, teaches how in the '90s and beyond we will be expected to work smarter, take better control of our health, adapt to advancing technology, and improve our lives in ways that are not too costly or resource-intensive. ($21.95 cloth)

SOMEONE ELSE'S SON, by Alan A. Winter, explores the parent-child bond in a contemporary story of lost identities, family secrets, and relationships gone awry. Eighteen years after bringing their first son home from the hospital, Trish and Brad Hunter discover they are not his natural parents. Torn between their love for their son, Phillip, and the question of whether they should help him search for his biological parents, the couple must also struggle with the issue of their own biological son. Who is he—and do his parents know their baby was switched at birth? ($18.95 cloth)

STRAIGHT TALK ON WOMEN'S HEALTH: How to Get the Health Care You Deserve, by Janice Teal, Ph.D., and Phyllis Schneider, is destined to become a health-care "bible" for women concerned about their bodies and their future health. Well-researched, but devoid of confusing medical jargon, this handbook offers access to a wealth of resources, with a bibliography of health-related books and contact lists of organizations, healthlines, and women's medical centers. ($14.95 paper)